PRAISE FOR *TEAM UP,*

Colleagues Cohan, Honigsfeld, and Dove show us the powerful possibilities that can and do happen when we work collaboratively with students, families, schools, and the community on behalf of English learners. They masterfully weave examples from the field to highlight current research-based approaches for co-creating a common purpose, shared mindset, supportive environment, and a diverse team that draws from the strengths and assets that everyone possesses. If you are seeking a book about collaborating on behalf of English learners' success, this should be a go-to reference.

—**Debbie Zacarian,** author, director of Zacarian and Associates

Another great book by Cohan, Honigsfeld, and Dove to reinforce the importance of teamwork in support of English language learners. The authors present a comprehensive framework that is woven throughout the book to encourage collaboration in the classroom, the school building, and the community. It is a must-read!

—**Carol Wertheimer,** educational consultant

Ensuring equitable access for all students requires collaborative efforts among educators, parents, and students. This thought-provoking book offers solutions to address critical issues of academic, language, and social-emotional learning that directly impact English learners' educational experiences.

—**Glenda Harrell, ESL director,** Wake County Public School System, NC

In their newest book, *Team Up, Speak Up, Fire Up!,* Audrey Cohan, Andrea Honigsfeld, and Maria G. Dove offer a fresh perspective on collaboration for ELLs/MLLs. Each chapter begins with a case study presenting the challenges inherent in this approach. By adhering to four core principles—common purpose, shared mindset, diverse team membership, supportive environment—the authors explain how these challenges can be overcome and how to successfully engage all stakeholders—administrators, teachers, students, parents, and community leaders—in the collaborative process.

—**Rochelle Verstaendig,** ENL teacher, former ENL coordinator, Plainview-Old Bethpage School District, professional development consultant, Nassau BOCES, NY

Collaboration is the central concept that is the running thread in this new book. Audrey, Andrea, and Maria bring us along a journey of thinking of collaboration in its different forms such as teacher–to–teacher, student–to–student, teacher–to–student, and teachers–to–community partnerships. Through each chapter, the authors weave in research that supports each form of collaboration, share commentary from educators who were able to form successful partnerships, and provide strategies to support collaboration whether it be with teachers, students, or the community. This book is the manual for anyone who has uttered the African proverb, "It takes a village to raise a child."

—**Tan Huyhn,** EAL teacher

Team Up, Speak Up, Fire Up! Educators, Students, and the Community Working Together to Support English Learners aligns with the pedagogical shifts that are required in order to move the needle for our English learners (ELs). One of the most valuable contributions to the field of second-language acquisition is the book's strong emphasis on teamwork and collaboration. We have found here in Beaverton that co-teaching is impossible to pull off without the consistent collaboration time between our English language development (ELD) teachers and classroom teachers. When teachers are able to consistently co-plan and co-assess with classroom teachers, we see increased collective efficacy among our professionals. What is more impressive is that students ultimately benefit and we have data to support that collaborative co-teaching, with heavy emphasis on collaboration, has a strong correlation to student achievement.

—**Toshiko Maurizio,** administrator for multilingual programs,
Beaverton School District, OR

Educators will find themselves eager to team up, speak up, and fire up as they read this powerful asset-based book on supporting English learners. The authors emphasize the value that diverse learners bring to schools and how everyone benefits when learning is inclusive. This book is an enabling tool for educators who are passionate about providing an equitable and engaging learning environment for English learners.

—**Lori M. Edmonds,** clinical assistant professor, University of North Carolina at Chapel Hill, School of Education, and president of Edmonds Educational Consulting, NC

How do you ensure ELs thrive in core classrooms? How do you ensure equitable access to asset-based, interactive, and authentically engaging learning? *Team Up, Speak Up, Fire Up!* This compelling guide helps educators apply concepts of effective teamwork to transform how students, teachers, leaders, and parents collaborate to ensure schools are affirming and empowering for multilingual learners.

—**Tonya Ward Singer**, author of *EL Excellence Every Day* and *Opening Doors to Equity*

Cohan, Honigsfeld, and Dove present a user-friendly and effective manual for teachers to embed collaborative structures into their daily classroom practices. They outline accessible and research-based strategies that will empower English learners to gain voice and an academic identity in the classroom setting. The book adds to the authors' already important contributions to the field of EL best practices, as well as teaching teachers to collaborate as a model for their students.

—**Ivannia Soto**, professor, Whittier College, CA

An essential key to EL student progress and success is the ability of all the surrounding adults to collaborate effectively. *Team Up, Speak Up, Fire Up!* not only provides solid systematic solutions to support various stakeholder collaboration, but the text also shares authentic real-life examples for all to learn from. An absolutely needed text to support and promote collaborative visions!

—**Tanya Franca,** director of ESOL, Greenville County Schools, SC

It's time for a book such as this! Its high energy establishes a blueprint for building effective teams while keeping the heart of the English learner at the forefront of a culture-rich mindset. A must-read for all teachers serving EL populations or EL program groups. Let this be your next team-building strategy for teachers of English learners.

—**Eileen Lockhart,** English learner professional development coordinator, Prince William County Schools, VA

Authors Cohan, Honigsfeld, and Dove do a fantastic job championing the power of purposeful collaboration in this must-have resource for educators who want guidance and support in leveraging teamwork for the benefit of English learners. Using four core principles of teamwork, they not only address how teacher teams can work collectively to engage in professional learning and problem solving, but also promote teamwork with a broader scope by addressing the power of student teams, teacher/student teams, and teams that involve community collaboration. This resource will certainly fire you up to embrace collaboration as an essential practice for enhancing outcomes of English learners.

—**Katie Toppel,** English language development specialist, Tigard-Tualatin School District, OR

As a professional developer, I look to Cohan, Honigsfeld, and Dove's work to enhance and deepen my own understanding of the latest thinking about English learners. This book offers a new framework for EL support based on teamwork. Cohan, Honigsfeld, and Dove now show you how these same core principles, when used within a supportive classroom and community environment, will lead to greater success for ELs. This book offers teachers a new guide with previously unexplored pathways for providing ELs (as well as other learners) with 21st century skills in both their classrooms and their communities. It also provides a road map—with explicit instructions and resources—to help ELs arrive successfully at their destination. Bravo, once again, to these authors!

—**Judy Dodge,** author and professional development consultant, NY

In their latest book, Cohan, Honigsfeld, and Dove team up, speak up, and fire up in their quest to support educators of English learners. Here, they bring together current research, authentic examples of best practices, and voices from the field, giving readers a treasure trove of resources that will undoubtedly empower them to support ELs and their families. Add this book to your PLC's reading list, and respond to their call to come together, collaborate, and advocate for inclusive school communities!

—**Gretchen Oliver,** assistant professor of education and assistant director of TESOL Programs, Clarkson University

I am delighted to have this wonderful book for our teachers of English learners! We know how important it is for all educators to work together in support of the English learners in their schools. In Massachusetts, as in other WIDA states, we value collaborative efforts between ESL teachers, special educators, and general education teachers. Our state's Department of Elementary and Secondary Education has developed an ESL curriculum design process, including the collaboration tool that guides us in these efforts, and this well-researched and highly readable book will support this work. The powerhouse writing team of Cohan, Honigsfeld, and Dove inspires us to also join forces, providing plenty of practical strategies for creating and maintaining our own powerful teams.

—**Bonnie Baer-Simahk,** ELL director, Fitchburg Public Schools, MA

Two of the areas that our district has focused on this year are "teamwork" and "transparency." Working together with all stakeholders helps us create a plethora of opportunities for our ELLs. It takes teamwork to improve practices and afford students with opportunities that once were only viewed as possibilities. Now we are making it happen and this new book will further support us in our efforts.

—**Wanda Ortiz,** assistant superintendent of bilingual services
K–12 and student intake, Brentwood, NY

TEAM UP SPEAK UP FIRE UP!

Educators, Students,
and the Community
Working Together to
Support English Learners

AUDREY **COHAN** / ANDREA **HONIGSFELD** / MARIA G. **DOVE**

ASCD | Alexandria, Virginia USA

1703 N. Beauregard St. • Alexandria, VA 22311-1714 USA
Phone: 800-933-2723 or 703-578-9600 • Fax: 703-575-5400
Website: www.ascd.org • E-mail: member@ascd.org
Author guidelines: www.ascd.org/write

Ronn Nozoe, *Interim CEO and Executive Director*; Stefani Roth, *Publisher*; Genny Ostertag, *Director, Content Acquisitions*; Susan Hills, *Acquisitions Editor*; Julie Houtz, *Director, Book Editing & Production*; Joy Scott Ressler, *Editor*; Judi Connelly, *Senior Art Director*; Thomas Lytle, *Graphic Designer*; Cynthia Stock, *Typesetter*; Kelly Marshall, *Interim Manager, Production Services*; Shajuan Martin, *E-Publishing Specialist*; Tristan Coffelt, *Production Specialist.*

PAPERBACK ISBN: 978-1-4166-2845-3   ASCD product #120004   n12/19
PDF E-BOOK ISBN: 978-1-4166-2847-7; see Books in Print for other formats.

Quantity discounts are available: e-mail programteam@ascd.org or call 800-933-2723, ext. 5773, or 703-575-5773. For desk copies, go to www.ascd.org/deskcopy.

Library of Congress Cataloging-in-Publication Data
Names: Cohan, Audrey, author.
Title: Team up, speak up, fire up!: educators, students, and the community working together to support English learners / by Audrey Cohan, Andrea Honigsfeld, and Maria G. Dove.
Description: Alexandria: ASCD, 2019. | Includes bibliographical references.
Identifiers: LCCN 2019023032 (print) | LCCN 2019023033 (ebook) | ISBN 9781416628453 (paperback) | ISBN 9781416628477 (pdf)
Subjects: LCSH: English language—Study and teaching—Foreign speakers. | Teaching teams.
Classification: LCC PE1128.A2 C655 2019 (print) | LCC PE1128.A2 (ebook) | DDC 428.0071—dc23
LC record available at https://lccn.loc.gov/2019023032
LC ebook record available at https://lccn.loc.gov/2019023033

28 27 26 25 24 23 22 21 20   1 2 3 4 5 6 7 8 9 10 11 12

We dedicate this book to all educators who team up, speak up, and fire up!

In memory of my dad, Norman Feinsilver, who understood the value of relationships.

Audrey Cohan

In appreciation of the Honigsfeld team—Howie, Ben, Jake, and Noah. You always inspire me to do more!

Andrea Honigsfeld

For my family—Tim, Dave, Jay, Sara, Christine, Meadow, Gavin, and Rohnan— who keep me grounded and remind me of what is most important.

Maria G. Dove

FOREWORD

Collaboration is the heart of relationship building, yet the historical precedent of isolationism of multilingual learners and their families from school has prevented the building of lasting partnerships. This chasm has left multilingual learners marginalized and disenfranchised in an educational system that has overlooked their valued contributions of language, culture, and identity to teaching, learning, and schooling. Until now. *Team Up, Speak Up, Fire Up!* underscores the importance of forming collaborative ties between and among educational stakeholders to promote their active engagement in forming an array of partnerships to support the growing numbers of multilingual learners and their families in the K–12 arena.

Shifting classroom, school, and community cultures to become more inclusive through teaming is a challenging undertaking. Having a principled framework that exemplifies the process facilitates this journey—and Cohan, Honigsfeld, and Dove have provided a framework! They have framed each chapter around the implementation of four core principles of teamwork— common purpose, shared mindset, supportive environment, and diverse team membership—by the most important educational stakeholders—students, teachers, and families. These building blocks for collaboration have been skillfully interwoven to yield a variety of partnerships that share a vision for continuous learning and lead to empowerment of multilingual learners, namely student–student, student–teacher, teacher–teacher, and teacher–school leader–community.

Partnership building begins at the micro level among students in classroom contexts. Student–student interaction between multilingual learners and their proficient English peers can readily become an integral part of the learning experience as language and content are seamlessly interwoven through student-generated discussion, whether in English, in the multilingual learners' shared partner language, or through translanguaging that accounts for the students' full linguistic repertoire. Having students rely on one another through reciprocal teaching facilitates their ownership in learning, strengthens their engagement, and promotes their agency. Ultimately, student–student collaboration results in the deepening of their personal learning and their ability to gain an understanding of our multicultural world.

Student–teacher relationships are also shifting, as instructional roles are being reshaped through teaming. With everyday participatory and interactive practices that occur in classrooms, both students and teachers can become inspired as they partake in the process of language development within content learning. Teachers, in partnering with students, take on a variety of roles—from mentors, to facilitators of learning, to that of curious learners and educators—to maximize multilingual learners' opportunities to learn, as students take on more responsibilities for learning.

Teacher–teacher teamwork has become more focused and deliberate as teacher pairs center on the planning of shared goals to enhance students' academic, literacy, linguistic, and socioemotional growth. The teaching-learning cycle also provides common ground for collaborative practices that entail teachers engaging in co-planning, co-teaching, and co-assessing. At a macro level of implementation, collaboration necessitates the building of relationships among school leaders, teachers, and families. Blurring the lines of delineation between educators and the communities served by schools facilitates the interchange of ideas and strategies. Additionally, highlighting the languages, cultures, and "ways of being" of the student body, along with their families, can cultivate the formation of school–community alliances.

Cohan, Honigsfeld, and Dove illustrate how moving across levels of implementation from student partnerships to teacher and leadership teams can lead to creating schoolwide conditions for systemic and lasting change. Their vision is to have collaboration become the facilitator for opening up lines of communication and trust to produce a pronounced synergy of practices that goes beyond classroom walls to embrace surrounding communities. In essence, these multilayers of collaboration aimed at championing multilingual learners and their families are essential ingredients for facilitating and maintaining a system of support. In each chapter, the visibility and feasibility of these collaborative efforts come to life in the myriad resources offered.

Collaboration builds trust and trust leads to building relationships, and relationships forge enduring partnerships throughout learning communities. Cohan, Honigsfeld, and Dove underscore the value of the cooperative nature of learning between teacher and learner in the broadest sense and the active roles of both in the process (Gibbons, 2015). Opening up and nourishing dialogue among the primary stakeholders of the educational community—students, teachers, and families—promotes team building (Team Up!) that fosters a shared mindset and voice (Speak Up!) to support advocacy and equity of multilingual learners (Fire Up!). Finally, there is a book that strives to make multilingual learners the centerpiece for creating and sustaining alliances to advance teaching and learning across educational settings.

Margo Gottlieb
May 2019

PREFACE

Team Up, Speak Up, Fire Up! offers practical strategies to build partnerships—between students and teachers, classroom teachers and specialists, families and educators, students and students—to uncover purposeful collaboration in support of English learners (ELs).

For too long, ELs have been segregated from their English-speaking peers or supported in a way that inadvertently led to isolation, limited access to the core curriculum, and exclusion from enriching language and learning opportunities. The tremendous assets that ELs bring to each school community are often unnoticed and misinterpreted as deficiencies. Their multiliteracies, resilience, lived experiences, and eagerness to learn must be recognized and nurtured through inclusivity. When teamwork becomes the norm in a school, ELs are better able to exercise their agency, more fully participate in all learning activities, and attain the self-efficacy of independent, critical thinkers.

In this book, we explore ways in which teachers, students, and communities benefit from research-based strategies and collaborative practices that result in enhanced outcomes for

ELs—who, in turn, develop a strong sense of belonging and confidence in shaping their academic futures.

OVERVIEW OF CHAPTERS

We will, in five chapters, make a compelling case for shifting the classroom, school, and community cultures toward the goal of making them more welcoming, fully engaging, and academically rewarding for ELs—and for all students! The cornerstone of making such shifts a reality is ... teamwork.

CHAPTER 1: THE POWER OF TEAMWORK

This chapter outlines a new framework for EL support in which teamwork is the foundation of the teaching-learning experiences within each classroom—and within and beyond the school. Rather than focusing on individuals and their personalities, differing experiences, and preferences, we showcase that successful teaming depends heavily on four core principles that form the foundation of our collaborative framework—common purpose, shared mindset, supportive environment, diverse team membership—and that essential building blocks—collaboration, continuous learning for all, and coordinated support for students, teachers, and families—are sustained.

CHAPTER 2: WINNING STUDENT TEAMS IN THE CLASSROOM

This chapter uncovers the power of a collaborative classroom culture, in which ELs learn alongside their English-speaking peers and frequently engage in interactive learning that integrates rigorous content with language and literacy development that enables ELs to better SWIRL—Speak, Write, Interact, Read, and Listen. Woven into the chapter are authentic examples that highlight a classwide comprehensive approach to best practices, which use the four core principles of our framework to support social-emotional development, academic learning, and language and literacy acquisition.

CHAPTER 3: TEACHERS AND STUDENTS ON THE SAME TEAM

This chapter presents practical, research-informed strategies to encourage teachers to relinquish full control of their classes and become facilitators and coaches of their students. This shift in instructional role supports students who engage in academic discoveries through problem solving as well as inquiry- and project-based learning that requires teamwork. Combining engagement and exploration with the four core principles that form the foundation of of teamwork creates a teacher–student partnership in which students develop ownership of their learning experiences.

CHAPTER 4: TEACHER TEAMS AT THEIR BEST

This chapter outlines a comprehensive approach to teacher teamwork that combines teacher expertise in nurturing the *entire* EL with ways of fostering students' academic, linguistic, literacy, and social-emotional growth. Using the four core principles of teamwork, teachers work together to design, implement, and reflect on curricular, instructional, and assessment practices that ensure success for ELs. Recognizing the importance of teachers' ongoing professional learning when implementing a new framework, this chapter offers specific ways to design, implement, assess, and sustain successful collaborative teaching practices.

CHAPTER 5: FIRED UP TO SUPPORT ELs: TEAMS THAT EXTEND BEYOND THE CLASSROOM

This chapter presents five key strategies for enhanced school, family, and community collaboration—create a safe and supportive learning environment, make resources and communication multilingual and multimodal, establish partnerships with community-based organizations, develop programs and activities that engage families and encourage advocacy and leadership, and share success stories to make success visible.

SPECIAL FEATURES

Chapters in *Team Up, Speak Up, Fire Up!* feature the following:

➤ *Opening vignettes* that highlight the complex challenges of real-life ELs in various contexts and that are revisited at the end of each chapter to synthesize ways that collaboration can be successful.

➤ *A revisiting of the core principles of our collaborative framework* and the presentation of the principles through the lens of each chapter (that is, student–student, teacher–student, teacher–teacher, and school–community partnerships).

➤ *Consider This.* Invitations to consider the various situations in which ELs find themselves and the struggles and challenges faced by many ELs, pushing your thinking in new directions related to the topic discussed.

➤ *Research to Watch.* Brief summaries of some seminal and current research that you may want to investigate further.

➤ *Key Terms.* Definitions of key terms to ensure a shared understanding of concepts surrounding collaboration.

➤ *See It in Action.* Translations of the ideas presented into practice.

➤ *Quick Tips.* Easy-to-try and ready-to-use strategies.

➤ *In Conversation with Teachers.* Conversations with teachers from around the United States who responded to the question, "How do you collaborate with ELs to impact student learning?"

➤ *Tech Toolbox.* Relevant technology tools that serve a collaborative purpose.

➤ *Taking It Further: Reflection Questions.* Questions that encourage continued dialogue and reflection.

➤ *Additional Resources.* A list of print and web-based resources for you to explore.

We invite you to continue this journey with us through the five chapters, which present the essential building blocks of sustained collaboration, continuous learning for ELs and their peers, and coordinated support for students, teachers, and families.

ACKNOWLEDGMENTS

This book would not have been possible without forming our own coauthoring team and being supported by a much larger team of dedicated professionals.

We would like to acknowledge all the educators who team up, speak up, and fire up on behalf of their English learners. Your contributions, which we are proud to showcase in this book, are powerful stories of advocacy and success with ELs.

A special thank-you goes to all our colleagues and friends at Molloy College, especially to Denise Hughes and Joyce Borelli. Many thanks to our doctoral research assistants, Jennifer Delahunt and Jenna Theofield, for their technical support.

We offer heartfelt thanks to those who offered their insightful feedback on an earlier version of this manuscript: Gretchen Oliver, Carol Salva, and Rochelle Verstaendig.

Last but not least, a sincere thank-you to our editor Susan Hills, who guided us through the entire ASCD publishing experience and whose patience, support, and collaboration are genuinely appreciated; and a heartfelt thank-you to our editor Joy Scott Ressler for her guidance in the detailed phases of book editing and production—her creativity and dedication to our vision were outstanding.

To all our readers, we thank you and applaud you for your courage and dedication to English learners and their families as you team up with colleagues and community members, speak up on behalf of some of the most vulnerable students, and fire up others to make a difference!

CHAPTER I

THE POWER OF TEAMWORK

"But all that we do is not enough."

Two weeks before the start of the new academic year, a large group of newly hired teachers spent the second morning of a three-day teacher orientation in conversations about the policies, programs, best practices, and resources concerning the school's large population of English learners (ELs). Their principal, Dr. Zoe Carrasco-Hernandez, began the morning meeting by outlining the federal, state, and local mandates for serving ELs; inviting discussions and feedback from the faculty; and sharing her strong commitment to careful curriculum planning and instructional designs for the success of this student population.

Dr. Carrasco-Hernandez recounted how she strives to create a welcoming environment for ELs and their families, beginning each day by greeting them in as many languages as possible as they enter the building alongside teachers and administrators and visiting a number

1

of classes each morning to have direct contact with teachers and students. She described how she instituted the use of a self-paced computer program for teachers and staff to develop basic communicative skills in languages other than English, and she even spoke a few sentences in Japanese to demonstrate her own progress in the program. Dr. Carrasco-Hernandez also shared how she maintains a collaborative decision-making philosophy and explained how she confers regularly with her teacher and leadership teams, as well as with parents and community leaders, with a particular emphasis on ELs. Then she paused for a moment and added, "But all that we do is not enough."

We wonder what the teachers must have been thinking, and how they might have been feeling, when Dr. Carrasco-Hernandez uttered, "But all that we do is not enough." Interestingly, what happened next came as quite a surprise to all in attendance.

Dr. Carrasco-Hernandez invited the new teachers to participate in a walking tour of the nearby community. The teachers, most of whom were unfamiliar with the neighborhood, walked together with the principal down to the main street in the town, and they all began to make selected stops at shops and businesses along the way. The teachers were impressed with how the community welcomed them as they walked alongside Dr. Carrasco-Hernandez and at how many people seemed to know the principal well. When the group returned to the building and settled in, Dr. Carrasco-Hernandez summarized their afternoon experience by simply saying, "Don't settle for simply what you can do with the students in your classroom or in this school; we—the administrators, faculty, and staff working together—must go into the greater community and must become an integral part of its fabric."

This book was born out of our passion and shared commitment over decades of our research, practice, and advocacy on behalf of ELs and their families. Our greatest takeaways from this commitment have been our interactions with many diverse people and their cultures, through which we have learned about their challenges and perseverance, hard work and commitment to education, beat-the-odds attitude often in the face of adversity, sense of community, and desire to learn. We have been humbled to see families who gave everything up to start their lives over for a better future for their children. Yet, we have always seen our work as a two-way street: we have dedicated our professional lives to English learners and have received so much more in return. Though we have written on this topic extensively, our goal is to offer our most compelling framework for advocacy and positive, authentic practices that will benefit ELs as well as all members of the school community. That's why the title of this book is *Team Up, Speak Up, Fire Up!*

THE ENGLISH LEARNER LANDSCAPE

Approximately 10 percent of all school-age children are English learners, with the highest concentration in California, Texas, Florida, New York, and Illinois, which combined total 60 percent of K–12 students (OELA, 2018). Ryan (2013) cited the 2011 Census Bureau data to report the top 10 languages spoken in U.S. households other than English are Spanish, Chinese, French, Tagalog, Vietnamese, Korean, German, Russian, Italian, and Portuguese. When looking at the top 10 languages spoken by English learners in the K–12 setting across the United States, a very different picture emerges, with the ranking being Spanish, Chinese, Arabic, Vietnamese, Haitian/Haitian Creole, Somali, Tagalog, Hmong, Portuguese, and Russian (Office of English Language Acquisition, 2017). Although language patterns in schools and heritage languages in neighborhoods may significantly vary from place to place, advocacy on behalf of multilingual communities must be a top priority.

SUCCESSFUL TEAMING AND COLLABORATION

Do you, as educators, ever wrestle with how to change the ways that many people feel about English learners and their families? When you work with colleagues or community members, do you focus on the individuals, their personalities, their different experiences and preferences, or the special synergy that emerges in the room? We have found that a team is always more than the sum of the individuals who make up the team.

We have also found that successful teaming depends heavily on four core principles that form the foundation of teamwork— common purpose, shared mindset, diverse team membership, and supportive environment. While there are many other contributing factors and variables that influence the formation of successful teams, these four principles help establish, build, and sustain teamwork from the bottom up. We derived these principles from multiple cross-referenced sources—the growing body of professional literature focusing on teaming, collaboration, and co-teaching, our collaborative research, and the practitioner knowledge and actions developed over decades of experience in the field of education. Writing this book has also been enriched through observing, interviewing, and interacting with successful collaborative educators—locally, regionally, nationally, and internationally—who generously shared their vast knowledge and transformative experiences about teamwork in support of ELs.

When we talk about teamwork in this chapter, we define collaboration and teaming in the broadest possible sense. In each community, we advocate for establishing shared goals of equity and access to the highest quality education for English learners.

As the National Education Association (2015) reminds us, *we all need to be in* to work collaboratively and effectively in service of a growing population of English language learners:

> English language learners deserve the same right to a great public school education as their English-speaking peers. They deserve access to a rich curriculum and validation of their home language and culture. They deserve educators who are trained to teach them, schools that welcome their families, and fair funding. They deserve an education community that shares a sense of urgency and responsibility for their well-being. They deserve the best we have to give them. These are America's students, and the nation can't afford to let them down. (p. 5)

In this book, we make the case for collaboration and show readers how to use it to provide access to high quality instruction and enriching learning experiences. English learners and their families need educators to work together. Therefore, consider this a call to *team up* to be fully inclusive and engage all students so they may live up to their unlimited potentials. Let's *speak up* when biases, prejudices, and deficits dominate the conversation and replace them with asset-based points of view and advocacy. Let's *fire up* others who might not yet recognize the strengths of all families and communities nor understand how this ever-growing student population is the future of our school systems. We need the talents, voices, and full participation of English learners.

WHY COLLABORATE?

Have you ever said or heard anyone say, "It's faster if I just do it by myself"? When you are in a rush, when the task seems formidable, when resources are short, when getting a team together may take longer than getting the job done, what is your default decision? Is it easier to work alone at times than get others on board? We recognize these feelings and reactions may apply to a range of personal and professional choices that we make every day. Yet, when we collaborate, we have instant access to others' ideas. Woodrow Wilson famously said, "I not only use what brains I have but all I can borrow." When we collaborate, we form a multilevel support system that

➤ Combines expertise,
➤ Nurtures new and creative ideas,
➤ Makes task completion more efficient and effective,
➤ Offers feedback on the process and outcomes,
➤ Enhances motivation, and
➤ Creates opportunities for reflection.

The list goes on, but to achieve all these outcomes, we need to intentionally create and sustain a support system, as impactful teamwork does not just happen by itself. We must add a focus on underserved or marginalized students—together, as a team—to provide these students and their families with unparalleled opportunities inside and outside of the classroom.

CONSIDER THIS

Have you ever thought of how members of the English learner community feel when

➤ A kindergartener walks into a new classroom where no one speaks her language and the sights and sounds feel overwhelming?
➤ A child walks into the cafeteria and nothing looks or smells familiar or even appetizing?
➤ A young man walks through the community and for the first time after taking some English classes, can read most of the store signs and street signs?
➤ The national headlines decry your race or religion with such frightening intensity that your family questions their decision to come to the United States?

➤ A refugee family arrives at the airport and is escorted to their new apartment, which was furnished by neighborhood parents and children they never met?

➤ A teacher becomes known in the community as a resource and trusted ally for navigating the home-to-school experience?

These examples may very well represent a cross-section of experiences that are common among immigrant children or children of immigrants and their families. The formidable task of responding to these challenges cannot fall on one person's shoulders. Rather, forming positive relationships and working in teams in the classroom, in the school, and in the larger community will create acceptance, plausible solutions to day-to-day challenges, a sense of belonging, and pathways to academic and linguistic success. Don't take our word for it. See the "Research to Watch" sections for examples of current findings on the importance of collaboration.

RESEARCH TO WATCH

➤ The National Education Association (NEA) (2015) reiterated their position statement from 50-odd years ago suggesting that there continues to be "a profound lack of urgency and understanding in the way in which schools perceive and educate ELL [English language learner] students" (p. 4). Yet, promising research reveals that through teacher collaboration, educators develop and embrace a shared responsibility for all learners.

➤ Epstein and Associates (2019) have been researching school–community partnerships for more than 30 years. They strongly recommend creating action teams for partnerships. Who should be on an action team? "Everyone with an interest in student success has a role to play in conducting productive partnership activities" (p. 87).

➤ Hattie (2015) has documented the importance of collaborative expertise among educators. He noted that a significant barrier to student learning is within-school variability. Meaningful teacher collaboration—such as shared exploration of successful instructional strategies, student data, and teaching practices—is imperative. When teachers collaborate, their collective efficacy—their belief in their shared effectiveness on impacting student outcomes—increases (Eells, 2011; Hattie, 2018).

🔑 SOME KEY TERMS

The selection of terms we are about to define may surprise you. Each of these words or phrases are commonly used in classroom and school contexts as well as in the larger educational community and beyond. As the following words—purpose, mindset, environment, diversity—are included as building blocks in our framework, we invite you to consider the following definitions:

➤ *Purpose.* An intention or goal that is meaningful, carefully planned, and designed to lead to actionable outcomes.
➤ *Mindset.* Implicit and explicit knowledge and understanding that impacts one's individual and collective actions.
➤ *Environment.* The context within which all teaching, learning, communication, and advocacy actions take place.
➤ *Diversity.* Various dimensions of identity that are shared characteristics among groups of people including, but not limited to, race, gender, LGBTQ identity, religion, ethnicity, culture, socioeconomic status, age, and ability.

When you hear these four words—purpose, mindset, environment, and diversity—what are the first images that come to mind? What other ideas do you associate with these words? For example, with the word *purpose*, did you think statements of purpose, which are frequently used as road maps within the field of education? How about *mindset*? Maybe you made a connection to Dweck's (2007) extensive work on distinguishing between fixed and growth mindsets. When you came across the term *environment*, did you equate learning environment with your classroom, school building, district, or community? We recognize that *diversity* is an all-encompassing buzzword in many spheres of life, from business to science to medicine. What dimension(s) of diversity popped into your mind in relation to your school: racial, ethnic, cultural, linguistic, gender, experiential, or something else? In this book, we do not claim to redefine these foundational concepts but rather validate your understanding and offer a unique perspective that helps define collaborative practices such as team building (team up!), communication (speak up!), and advocacy (fire up!).

 ## QUICK TIP 1: SPEAK THE SAME LANGUAGE!

Spend some time with your colleagues in conversation to unpack some of the key terms. Do we really see eye to eye when we use terms such as *purpose* and *diversity*? Put these terms on your agenda at the next department or schoolwide meeting to discuss and share different perspectives. Also, invite colleagues to consider how these essential ideas have affected your English learners.

THE FOUR CORE PRINCIPLES OF TEAMWORK

The four core principles of teamwork—common purpose, shared mindset, diverse team membership, and supportive environment—serve as the foundation for the day-to-day work with students, fellow teachers, administrators, parents, family, and community members. While we defined purpose, mindset, environment, and diversity, we designed a framework that unifies the four core principles of teamwork (see Figure 1.1), which require deep exploration.

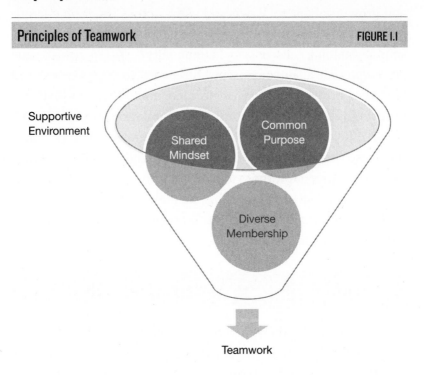

Principles of Teamwork   FIGURE 1.1

Teamwork doesn't just happen. Context, intentions, and actions matter. Teamwork is dependent upon the interaction of essential components including (1) the establishment of a *common purpose*, (2) the development of *shared mindset*, and (3) ensuring *diverse membership*. These three ingredients thrive in a *supportive environment* in which all stakeholders team up, speak up, and fire up!

COMMON PURPOSE

What is at the core of education? How do you define the purpose of schooling? There might be competing schools of thought and philosophies of education, and not all educators or members of the larger education community will agree on every detail, yet one point is clear: For teams of people to work together effectively, they must have a shared mission with the purpose of maintaining high academic standards and full inclusion to empower all students. Working toward establishing a common purpose and shared mission, teams and their members will

➤ Contribute to their fullest capacity.

➤ Work willingly and intentionally to meet clearly established goals or norms of participation.

➤ Welcome new ideas and maintain an openness to others' points of view.

➤ Collaboratively develop a shared focus on students' academic, linguistic, social, emotional, and physical growth.

➤ Prioritize continuous improvement of all aspects of collaboration among students, educators, and community members.

SHARED MINDSET

When you first meet English learners, how do you describe them? How do you and your colleagues define success for these youngsters? Tung (2013) reminds us not to view "ELL [English language learner] education as a problem, dilemma, achievement gap, or crisis"; instead, she urges us to "embrace ELLs as the very community members who, when well educated, will be the bicultural, bilingual leaders who improve our . . . neighborhoods and help us participate effectively in the global economy" (p. 4). Both individually and collectively, we must have an asset-based—rather than deficiency-oriented—mindset when it comes to culturally and linguistically diverse learners and their families. We must also have a shared responsibility for all students in our care and help every person—child, educator, family, and community member associated with the school—to thrive. To achieve this, team members must

➤ Embrace the challenge of defining success for all and creating a shared mindset around ELs.

➤ Examine biases and prejudices that focus on deficits rather than assets.

➤ Have a coherent and comprehensive vision for excellence and equity for all.

➤ Recognize cultural, linguistic, and academic assets of students, their families, and communities, value them and consistently build upon them.

➤ Share the collective message and unapologetically engage in dialogue and difficult conversations.

DIVERSE TEAM MEMBERSHIP

Teams require diverse membership in order to represent diverse perspectives and diverse voices from the school and the larger community. The challenge may be to bring people together from all walks of life and create cohesion and shared goals. You might begin by asking who the teammates should be to best represent English learners and keep their unique needs in mind. As facilitating well-balanced teams may not be easy, here are some suggestions to get started:

➤ Think about how each team member might bring a different perspective to the team.

➤ Aim for transparency so that the team knows what they will accomplish, and write down the goals or objectives so everyone can see them.

➤ Include members who understand the school's history regarding ELs and who are familiar with previous initiatives.

➤ Include people who don't think like you, don't look like you, and whose experiences differ from yours.

➤ Offer teaming as a way for everyone to have a voice.

Core principles remain just principles if we don't act on them. A first step to translate principles into actions is to ask key questions, reflect, and plan action steps. See Figure 1.2 for guiding questions related to the four core principles. In the last column,

Guiding Questions Related to the Four Core Principles   FIGURE I.2

Core Principles	Guiding Questions	Additional Questions and Possible Action Steps to Take
Common Purpose	What do you hope to accomplish through collaboration for your ELs and their families?	
Shared Mindset	What information/data do you need, and how do you make collective sense of it to lead to actionable decisions on behalf of ELs and their families?	
Diverse Team Membership	Why do you need diversity among team members, and how do you make sure members are committed to respecting, inviting, appreciating, and advocating for diversity?	
Supportive Environment	How do you ensure shared ownership and a sense of belonging that promotes team building (team up!), communication (speak up!) and advocacy (fire up!)?	

we invite you to generate additional questions and action steps applicable to your local context related to each core principle to further support your collaborative efforts. We have found that the most successful examples of collaborative practices on behalf of ELs take place in schools, districts, and communities where there is a strong sense of commitment and local ownership of partnerships that occur between and among stakeholders such as students, educators, parents, and community members.

SUPPORTIVE ENVIRONMENT

Energizing teams within and between teachers, students, families, and communities demands a supportive and accommodating environment. Think about your grade, your school, and your district and ask yourself whether it is an environment in which teams *thrive*. Some teams will develop and flourish with minimal encouragement. Other teams will require supports, structures, and protocols to create sustainable and effective units. All teams need resources—human and professional capital as well as financial resources—to succeed. Begin by thinking about how you will rally for English learners within your context and how to secure additional resources for them. How can you accomplish this?

➤ Create structures and logistical support for working together.

➤ Engage in open communication and take risks when defining short- and long-term goals.

➤ Mirror the support shown by leadership as well as foster support from all stakeholders.

➤ Have inside-out and outside-in commitment.

➤ Value advocacy and everyone's potential in a future-oriented context.

➤ Design ways to invite others to the "table" and define how you will work as a group and enhance learning opportunities for English learners.

⏱ QUICK TIP 2: START SMALL!

Creating a high-functioning, highly effective team takes time and effort as well as personal and collective commitment. Focus on the core—the core principles and a core group of people. When we visit schools and work directly with educators, we suggest a two-by-two approach: set two goals, form partnership with two people at a time, and engage in two actions with observable and measurable outcomes!

SEE IT IN ACTION

Have you ever heard a colleague say something like this: "Some of my ELs are doing really well in school! I wonder how I can get to know and support other English learners just as well." The first step is building a team, and the second step is ensuring robust communication with active partners. The third step is advocacy through partnerships and networks with families and communities.

TEAM UP: TEAM BUILDING

Have you ever participated in an icebreaker with the goal of team building? Some of our favorites are the Scavenger Hunt, Five Common Things, and Two Truths and a Lie. Although you may or may not enjoy these games, we can agree that, in most cases, these group activities work. What do they accomplish, and how do they achieve their goal? Team-building games typically

➤ Allow people to introduce themselves and share something about their lives,

➤ Highlight commonalities among people,

➤ Create a relaxed, safe environment,

➤ Set the ground rules for respectful interactions, and

➤ Are a good way to begin to foster relational trust.

Most important, opportunities for breaking down barriers and building new connections emerge on the spot. The challenge is to scale this up and not stop at icebreakers and game-like group activities. In the current educational context, educators, students, and parents can no longer work in isolation. We know that successful schooling experiences require a joint, coordinated effort; creative collaboration; and opportunities for enrichment that mirror real life.

A team is always more than the sum of the individuals who make up the team. To get started with team building and to make your team more effective, consider the work of Tuckman

(1965), a psychology professor at Ohio State University. He first introduced his framework of team development half a century ago, and many others have produced variations on it (for example, see Bonebright, 2010). We find that Tuckman's descriptions of forming, storming, norming, and performing continue to be a most useful frame of reference for understanding how to team up to support ELs!

Forming. Begin with creating a group that commits to working toward the same goal—in this case, to support and advocate for ELs. In this early stage of your team developing, team members should agree upon the expectations for what your team can accomplish, and the excitement should be building for future endeavors and achievements.

Storming. This is when the real works starts. Your goals and expectations may need to be broken down into chunks or achievable tasks and assigned to members. This is the "how to get it done" stage of teaming, and members must work together and share ideas and concerns.

Norming. At this point, your team should be examining successes and increasing productivity. This is a good time for team members to reflect on their progress and evaluate the goals developed previously. The team should be enjoying the work and one another and may even be socializing.

Performing. Your team has taken giant steps toward the goals; expectations and commitment should be high. All team members know their tasks and roles and may begin to switch with other members as overall competency on the team grows.

SPEAK UP: COMMUNICATION

"Our lives begin to end the day we become silent about the things that really matter" is an anonymous quote frequently attributed to Dr. Martin Luther King, Jr.; no doubt it was inspired by his own words and activism. In school communities, as in life in general, speaking up can at times subject the speaker to many risks. Ask newly employed teachers, untenured faculty, or educators who are up for a promotion or a new position about the likelihood of publicly sharing their opinions on school matters, and they might tell you how frequently they have been given advice by colleagues and mentors about when to use their voices and when to remain silent. Teachers commonly become concerned about speaking up when sensitive subjects are being discussed in the open or when their opinions might not align with those of the administration or board of education.

Today, maybe more than ever before, participation in difficult conversations about immigration, immigrant children, and children of immigrants are met with some reticence and apprehension. Many educators may not want to be singled out for what might be unwelcome points of view. Yet, the success of English learners often depends on the brave actions of educators, no matter their stages in their careers, and brave actions often require bucking the system at some point in order for all needed voices to be heard.

To encourage educators to use their voices, we would like to frame professional communication and collaboration by highlighting the types of conversations that can further the success of speaking up for the sake of diverse students and their families:

➤ *Confidential conversations.* You may not always be ready to share your thoughts, ideas, or opinions in public arenas. However, you may feel comfortable having conversations with close colleagues or sympathetic school leaders who are able to bring pressing issues, such as the challenges unaccompanied minors face, to light. Alternatively, consider having confidential conversations with union or faculty representatives who sit on particular committees, or who are in positions that allow them to, or who are willing to give voice to your concerns and recommend further actions.

➤ *Coordinated conversations.* To bring issues to the greater school community, regularly scheduled meetings in which community members coordinate their requests for the same item or items to be added to meeting agendas is another way to bring forth topics for discussion without having a spotlight shone on one person. To make this work, you will need a small group of dedicated faculty and staff who will promote and support the larger conversation about select issues (such as assigning fair and meaningful homework to English learners).

➤ *Compelling conversations.* These types of conversations often spring from seize-the-moment or compelling ideas in response to a local event or incident that brings complex issues to the forefront. When there is an urgent need to address what is happening in the school or larger community (e.g., symbols of religious or ethnic defamation appearing in public spaces), invite others to contribute so that the largest group of stakeholders can have a seat at the table.

➤ *Courageous conversations.* Glenn Singleton committed the Pacific Education Group, founded in 1992, to achieving racial equality through Courageous Conversations™, an effective protocol promoting interracial dialogue. Our intention here is similar but much broader in scope to include any conversations that require determination, fearlessness, and endurance from discussion participants to speak truth to power in order to bring to the forefront issues that affect culturally and linguistically diverse students and their families and to transform mindsets and behaviors. Think about a range of ways in which ELs' civil rights might be violated unintentionally or the detrimental impact of federal and state guidelines (for instance, ELs must be serviced with adequate, highly qualified staff without unnecessary practices of segregation [U.S. Department of Justice & U.S. Department of Education, 2015] that are not followed.

We call on all educators to use their voices to provide accurate information supported by evidence, to share their truth in the best way people will hear it, to listen well to all those concerned, and to go to the conversation whenever possible and wherever it may be—in the classroom, in the school, in the district, in the greater community, and beyond—to speak up for English learners!

⏱ QUICK TIP 3: TRY LESSON STUDY!

As early as the 1970s, teachers recognized that working collectively, or in teams, would benefit lesson planning, promote instructional change, and benefit students. Have you ever participated in joint lesson planning, co-planning, or the lesson-study model adopted from Japan (Lewis & Hurd, 2011), the purpose of which is to engage in honest communication about what works and what needs improvement? When we support lesson-study initiatives, it leads to a shared community of teachers who become more vested in designing the high-quality lessons for their students. So, if you or a colleague are facing an educational problem or are having difficulty designing lessons that reach all students—including ELs—consider the lesson-study professional-development model that is built on the concept of teams participating in collegial conversations.

FIRE UP: ADVOCACY

More than a decade ago, Crawford (2008) stated that "Decisions on how to teach English learners are being made not in the classroom, but in legislative chambers and voting booths; not on the basis of educational research data, but on the basis of public opinion, often passionate but uninformed" (p. 59). What has changed over the last 10–12 years? What do we know about best practices for ELs? We believe that strong advocacy on behalf of these learners is a nonnegotiable. All stakeholders must have a clear understanding of the academic, linguistic, socio-cultural, curricular, and instructional needs of ELs and how to best respond to them. Advocacy means being their voice when needed and lifting their voices so they are heard.

Within her advocacy framework, Staehr Fenner (2013a) invites educators to reflect on a series of self-evaluation questions focusing on equitable education for ELs. One essential question is whether ELs have "access to a challenging, high-quality, and developmentally appropriate curriculum aligned to the state's standards within and across content areas" (p. 87). EL specialists alone cannot ensure such access. All teachers must work together to create culturally and linguistically responsive and sustaining educational opportunities during the school day and beyond. Staehr Fenner proposes a cycle of reflection and action, which inspired us to generate the following guiding questions:

➤ What are your beliefs about and expectations of ELs?
  ➤ What do you know about your students' backgrounds and lived experiences?
  ➤ What informs your beliefs about ELs?
  ➤ In what ways are your beliefs asset- or deficiency-oriented?
  ➤ Do you have an accurate assessment of what your ELs can *do*?
  ➤ To what degree are your academic expectations impacted by school, district, and state policy and regulations?

➤ What is your own cultural background, and how does it influence how you teach?

> How much do you share about your identity with your students?

> Does your upbringing and own schooling experiences impact your teaching practices and your expectations for your students?

> Do you recognize if there is a cultural and experiential mismatch between your own life and those of your students? If so, what do you do about it?

➤ What personal and professional experiences have you had that help build empathy for ELs and their families?

> Have you had any authentic experiences with culturally and linguistically diverse communities that helped you become an advocate?

> Have you had formal training in culturally and linguistically responsive and sustaining pedagogy?

> Have you had any opportunities to request or to design professional learning opportunities that deepen your knowledge and sharpen your skills?

➤ How do you develop a shared responsibility with your colleagues on behalf of ELs?

> When you contribute to curricular and instructional decisions (including policymaking), how do you take into account the cultural, linguistic, and lived experiences of all of your students?

> Do you work in a professional learning community (PLC) or any other professional, collaborative learning structure?

> Are you committed to the notion of advocacy? If so, what individual and collective actions do you take?

Here's an example of a team formation in action that incorporates all three dimensions of our work:

Forming. A small group of educators visit the local community center and speak with the families about preparing for school. They want to introduce themselves, get to know the incoming kindergarteners and their families, and find out ways that educators in the local school and the community can work together. The discussion focuses on how to build on community assets, how to provide community-based resources for all children to enhance access to early childhood education, and how to offer school resources to parents who do not want to or cannot enroll their children in early childhood programs. (Team up!)

Storming. The group discusses ways to prepare for kindergarten by introducing games parents can play at home, Spanish/English books they can read, storytelling, and other activities they can engage in with the children prior to fall enrollment. They brainstorm a series of make-and-take workshops to be offered for parents and family members (e.g., older siblings). The librarian sets up a lending library at the community center, and teachers take turns volunteering to lead family story time at 4:00 every Monday and Wednesday. Parents, who are encouraged to get library cards, go to the library along with a 2nd grade teacher who lives in the community and is well known and trusted by many. Backpacks with materials for kindergarten (picture books, scissors, paper, pencils, crayons, basic cut-and-paste activities) donated by a local business are handed out (and many more can be borrowed on a rotating basis). The team discusses ways to scale the model for other elementary schools. (Speak up!)

Norming. The team meets several times a month with clear agendas to evaluate the progress and assess their goals. The level of collaboration and enthusiasm is high, and the group is considering periodically meeting with school and district leadership to report on their progress. Another goal is added to the objectives focused on the enrichment of language. Activities become more targeted as more kindergarten teachers join the team to share information regarding the skills that kindergarteners are expected to develop. Authentic stories of success are shared with the entire team and the community. Small groups are formed to prepare bookbags and have one-on-one meetings with the new parents who need help and have questions about navigating the community and the school system. After having recruited a bilingual parent liaison, parent groups are held at the community center—and now at the school as well—to discuss ways to develop language, literacy, and numeracy skills at home with both the home language and English. A name for the program has been established, and community members recommend the program to recent arrivals. (Speak up more!)

Performing. The team has entered into its third year, and kindergarten teachers enthusiastically report that school readiness has increased among children who attended early childhood programs and those who joined the community center's early education group. The group looks at the data for the number of children who participated in the activities in the community center and consider applying for a grant to scale the program and develop outreach protocols. Mostly, the program has succeeded because of the positive collaboration between the school district and the community center. Many team members note that the plan needs to be formalized. The team members have remained consistent, with only a few members leaving the group due to employment changes or for personal reasons. The team members have established a Facebook page with a growing number of followers and group chat for easy communication. (Fire up!)

IN CONVERSATION WITH TEACHERS

We asked educators around the country the following question: How does leadership support a profoundly collaborative school culture? Here are some compelling answers we received. As you read them, consider how they can help inform your practice.

Karen C. Woodson, Ph.D., principal of Mary Harris "Mother" Jones Elementary School, in Adelphi, Maryland, shared her own journey as an instructional leader to initiate a transformative change:

> *The first challenge to charting a path to school improvement for a high-impact Title 1 elementary school was to determine how the school's 13 ESOL teachers were being used to create schoolwide conditions for students to learn grade-level content and academic English simultaneously. Drawing on my background in district-level ESOL program leadership, I immediately set out to answer the following questions: What models of ESOL instruction were in place and how did ESOL teachers determine what types of supports would be used? What curricula were being used to provide ESOL instruction? How much time was being dedicated to ESOL instruction? How were caseloads determined for each ESOL teacher?*
>
> *The answers to these questions revealed a deep level of variance that would block any effort for systemic school improvement. For example, each individual ESOL teacher determined which ESOL instructional model to use to serve his or her students. ESOL teachers also varied in their approach to the curriculum, which resulted in inequitable and sporadic access to grade-level content. Teachers also varied in the amount of ESOL instruction provided to students at different English language proficiency levels. The only area of consistency was that students were assigned to ESOL teachers in equal numbers, resulting in ESOL teachers working across grade levels.*
>
> *To minimize variance and increase equitable access to grade-level curriculum, we shifted the role of the ESOL teacher to one that focused on creating schoolwide conditions for learning academic English through grade-level content. This meant that two ESOL teachers were*

assigned to each grade level, regardless of the number of ELs in the grade, enabling them to become experts in grade-level curriculum and full-fledged members of the grade-level teams to which they were assigned. Pull-out instruction was limited to beginning-level ESOL students. ESOL teachers and grade-level teachers deepened professional learning around differentiation of grade-level curriculum and the provision of explicit, content-based English language development instruction.

The key to this shift has been a deep commitment to teacher-led professional learning around collaboration and co-teaching in grade-level teams. Equally important was creating the space for ESOL teachers to form their own community of practice around building their capacity to provide structured, systematic English language development instruction steeped in grade-level content. This EL-centered, teacher-led improvement strategy forms the core of our school improvement effort. I am optimistic that greater numbers of our students will be able to achieve proficiency in academic English and meet or exceed grade-level, college-, and career-readiness standards.

Esmeralda Carini, content literacy specialist at the Kailua/ Kalaheo Complex in Hawaii, described how she provided leadership to support teacher collaboration:

Teachers' and administrators' personal and professional learning are too often isolated from their practice. Many do not have the opportunity to share and reflect with other practitioners on problems of practice or to grow innovative ideas on an ongoing basis. Learning communities allow for educators to tap into the expertise within the school through coaching, mentoring, and knowledge sharing. However, providing a structure for a learning community to occur is not enough. I believe that in order to encourage and enable effective teaching practices for the 21st century, schools must commit to ongoing, job-embedded, differentiated professional learning opportunities for their staff wrapped within a community of practice (CoP).

We also know that teacher learning requires collaboration (social interaction) in trusting environments where they feel supported to take a series of risks in order to grow their practice. This type of "risk taking" is not always easy to do on the job and requires support. When reflecting on my own practice, some of the deepest learning I have experienced has been when I felt supported by a group of individuals who shared similar goals, who learned and practiced alongside me, and who had a vested interest in seeing me succeed. One could call this learning within a community of practice.

As a district content literacy specialist, I felt the urgency to create a professional learning structure, Hawaii Lab Cohorts (HLC), that would enhance teachers' content knowledge and pedagogy to a level where they would feel confident enough to become change agents at their schools. As a literacy leader, I believe that it is my responsibility to ensure that teachers' learning opportunities are situated in authentic experiences and are differentiated to support individually chosen goals within a CoP. It is also imperative that I model and engage in the professional learning alongside my lab teachers. This gives value to the knowledge that we all bring to our profession and creates stronger learning communities at our schools for both educators and their students to flourish.

Nina "Will" Williams, director of the Multilingual Education Department, Kent School District, Washington, shared her district's strategy to establish teacher leadership roles to enhance collaboration for ELs:

> *One of the most effective structures we have put in place to support this work districtwide is a cadre of collaborative teaching lead teachers. After hosting initial districtwide workshops about co-teaching, the multilingual education team asked principals to identify their most dynamic teacher leaders, who would participate in a year-long coaching and training cycle to prepare them to deliver professional learning and assist in managing collaborative teaching implementation in their schools. We ended up with a wonderful mix of classroom teachers, EL specialists, and instructional specialists from every school and from all grade levels and disciplines. The team comes together monthly to share, learn, support one another, and plan together for successful implementation. Our collaborative teaching team has been meeting for eight months now, and we are building an amazing team of professionals dedicated to collaborative practice. Having a multitude of perspectives coming together to inform and enrich our collective efforts toward improving instruction for English learners has been an amazing asset. Collaborative teaching leads is a structure we want to continue to develop and sustain.*

⏱ QUICK TIP 4: CELEBRATE SUCCESSES AND LEARN FROM CHALLENGES!

At the end of the school day, share with a colleague or team member one of your success stories. Do you ever go home thinking about what did not go well? If so, why not instead use reflection as a powerful tool and pat yourself on the back by sharing a success story, even the seemingly small ones? When working with English learners, the growth in language proficiency may be gradual, so you need to listen or read carefully and energize the teachers around you to recognize accomplishments.

🧰 TECH TOOLBOX

Make use of technology tools and online resources that support building collaborative school and community cultures.

SCHOOL AND CLASS WEBSITES

School websites provide essential information to the community about registration, curriculum, meetings, special events, school closings, and so on. Class websites are specific to individual course content and give parents particular news about overall student learning, class assignments, and other pertinent information. Facebook, Weebly, and Wix are the most commonly available and free platforms to create web pages and websites that keep families informed. These platforms can be used in the most creative ways, including livestreaming school events or even reading a nighttime story to early childhood students (see Belinda Georgei, principal of Homer Drive Elementary School in

Beaumont, in Southeast Texas: https://www.facebook.com/pg
/HomerScholars/videos/?ref=page_internal).

YOUTUBE CHANNEL

Developing a YouTube Channel, on which you can post video
content of school and neighborhood activities involving students, can really draw families into the life of a district. It is one of
the best ways to promote good will and engagement among members of the greater school community—and it's free! Northern
Parkway School in Uniondale, New York, uses a Youtube channel
to communicate with the parents and the community—https://
www.youtube.com/channel/UCimKpMsGSwIK4IGRyVN_qaA.

REMIND

Remind, an interactive platform for communication, is a powerful tool often used by teachers and administrators to manage
communication with families and encourage community engagement. A message can be delivered via the app, SMS, or e-mail
and can be sent by a principal, teacher, or coach. In the event
that school is closed due to inclement weather or a basketball
game has been rescheduled, Remind provides an easy means of
communication. Audio recordings can be used to share school
events with a parent who may be working, giving them the opportunity to feel like they were present.

CONCLUSION

The goal of this chapter was to offer the foundational understandings of teaming in support of ELs. Successful teamwork is
dependent upon essential elements such as common purpose
(the development of a mission embraced by all), shared mindset (a collective vision), and diverse membership that invites
active contributions from multiple, varied perspectives. Teaming

thrives in a supportive environment in which commitment, risk taking, open communication, and advocacy are valued. So, we must team up, speak up, and fire up!

Taking It Further: Reflection Questions

1. In what ways are you already collaborating with your students, their families, and the local community? Building on this foundation, what next steps might you take to strengthen these bonds and provide coordinated support inside and outside of the classroom?
2. What cultural frames of reference do you have, and how do you learn more about your students' lived experiences?
3. How do you validate your students' cultures and acknowledge their home lives? How can this be a building block for communication and advocacy in the future?

Additional Resources

Are you familiar with all the legal obligations as well as federal guidelines when it comes to serving English learners? The Office of English Language Acquisition created (and recently updated) the *English Learner Toolkit*, which has all the information you need to get started. Visit https://www2.ed.gov/about/offices/list/oela/english-learner-toolkit/index.html.

Are you looking for the most up-to-date research on English learners? The Center for Applied Linguistics has an elaborate website that shares extensive research-based professional development and disseminates resources related to both language and culture. Visit http://www.cal.org/areas-of-impact/english-learners.

Have you followed any high-quality blogs that offer authentic teaching suggestions for teachers of ELs? An award-winning website by Larry Ferlazzo is like a one-stop shop for ideas when teaching English learners. Mr. Ferlazzo is a prolific writer of books as well as blogs, and you will find his work relevant and timely. Visit http://larryferlazzo.edublogs.org.

CHAPTER 2

WINNING STUDENT TEAMS IN THE CLASSROOM

After conversations with colleagues, she realized that the approach would prove effective—and contagious!

Annalise Vincent, a mid-career English teacher at Lincoln Elementary School, began the new school year by attending several professional development workshops at her district's Superintendent's Conference Day, held on the morning before classes were to begin. At one workshop, she was soon to learn that a new initiative to address the oral and written discourse of English learners (ELs) was about to be launched at her school. Subsequently, Ms. Vincent and her 5th grade colleagues would be charged with finding more frequent and better opportunities for their students—including ELs who spoke little or no English—to increase their peer-to-peer interactions.

While Ms. Vincent considered herself to be open-minded, the suggestions she heard at this workshop made her skeptical, hesitant, and downright concerned. The number of challenges she typically had in any one of her classes—students with various levels of English proficiency, struggling readers, and several students with disabilities, coupled with large class sizes—frequently guided the choices she made to manage her classes. Traditional teaching methods—direct instruction, students who listened and observed, and independent seatwork— were the go-to learning strategies she most frequently used to cover a rigorous curriculum, gather assessment data, and monitor student behavior.

To comply with the new directive, Ms. Vincent decided to initiate one new strategy—turn and talk. She would have students complete a Do Now or some type of independent seatwork, and at the culmination of the task, she would ask students to team up with a nearby student to discuss their completed work. Ms. Vincent would set a timer and allow students one minute to converse. When the buzzer sounded, she would invite teams of students to share what they had heard. After several weeks, Ms. Vincent noted that her students seemed to enjoy the interactions they shared; yet she was unsure of the impact such activities were having on student learning.

After conversations with colleagues, she realized that the approach would prove effective—and contagious! At the end of the second month of the new school year, Ms. Vincent met with her 5th grade colleagues in their designated monthly grade-level meeting. After addressing routine matters—school policies on birthday celebrations, collection of money for an upcoming school trip, problems with student behavior during recess, and so on—she told colleagues about the positive preliminary results she was getting in her classroom. The newest member of the team, James Palma, began to share his own experiences with planning lessons with the new initiative in mind—grouping students for instruction.

Mr. Palma, a third-year teacher, had embraced the idea of students working collaboratively and developed opportunities for teamwork with a 5th grade social studies unit on how different ethnic, social, and religious groups contributed to the culture of the United States. He enthusiastically reported how he configured students to explore different perspectives of events and issues, supported ELs to analyze authentic documents, and fostered their motivation to work in small groups by tapping into their personal interests. He shared how all his students exceeded his expectations for meeting the unit's objectives and even bragged a little about how well they performed on the summative unit test.

At first, Mr. Palma's keen interest and excitement were given a tepid reception by team members. What the others on the team had tried as far as initiating an increase in student interaction were attempted and reported with mixed results. However, Ms. Vincent, an emerging teacher leader on this 5th grade team, was intrigued by Mr. Palma's results and wanted to continue to grow her own practice with this new approach. She began to ask pointed questions about his grouping practices and turned the discussion into a brainstorming session on student-centered work. During this time, a few teachers grabbed their iPads and searched websites for ideas and resources for students to work cooperatively. Mr. Palma convinced a few colleagues to embrace the new idea and then others followed. By the end of the session, everyone agreed to explore one new strategy for increasing their students' oral or written discourse through group work with the plan to share their successes and challenges during their next team meeting.

In Chapter 1, we made a compelling case for building teams (large and small) and taking a collaborative approach to educating all students. We emphasized that combining individuals' (whether teachers', administrators', parents', or students') knowledge, skills, and willingness to create caring, supportive, learning opportunities will lead to success for English learners.

In this chapter, we transfer what we presented previously as the four core principles of teamwork to the classroom level and show how common purpose, shared mindset, diverse team membership, and supportive environment are also the key ingredients of a collaborative classroom culture. As you read through this chapter, you will uncover the power of the SWIRL-ing classroom—one in which ELs learn alongside their English-speaking peers and frequently engage in interactive learning that integrates rigorous content with language and literacy development. Students *S*peak, *W*rite, *I*nteract, *R*ead, and *L*isten—SWIRL—while they collaborate with each other, resulting in supporting students' social-emotional development, academic learning, and language and literacy acquisition.

WHY FORM STUDENT GROUPS?

Think back to your elementary or secondary years as a student. We are most confident, unfortunately, that you have had at least a few teachers who stood in front of your class, lectured a lot (and that means just about all the time), and did not even realize that you and some of your friends stopped paying attention and retained little of what was presented. In the years you have spent teaching or learning to teach, you've likely heard or even used the terms "chalk and talk," "sage on the stage," and "talking head" to describe a style of teaching that puts the teacher front and center. These less-than-flattering terms do not even capture how little learning might take place and what students truly experience in classes that are dominated by teacher talk. When Sousa (2016) said, "Whoever explains, learns!" (p. 107), we knew his intention was not to endorse your teachers from yesteryear. Instead, he suggested we need to give all students a chance to get very good at making sense of what they are learning and explaining what they have learned. If students are prepared to teach others, they have certainly developed mastery. This kind of powerful learning experience can be maximized in collaborative student groups. Figure 2.1 presents an anchor chart designed to help students with academic discourse. Sentence starters and prompts guide English learners with the type of academic oral language that is needed for successful classroom participation. In the example in the figure, the anchor chart supports student

Anchor Chart for Academic Discourse FIGURE 2.1

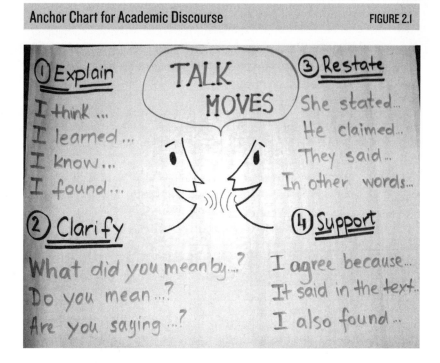

language use related to four critical language tasks—explain, restate, clarify, and support.

In a successful and productive independent learning situation, teachers listen for the simultaneous use of academic language, literacy skills, and rigorous content (Dove, Honigsfeld, & Cohan, 2014). A productive small group will have *all* students interacting with one another to build upon each other's knowledge. English learners thrive when they have opportunities to share their prior knowledge, showcase their expertise (Brown, 2010) and their funds of knowledge (Moll, Amanti, Neff, & Gonzalez, 1992), and build academic capital that may differ from what other students possess.

CONSIDER THIS

Think of the complexities of language and literacy development:

➤ As a baby or young child, you have mastered a very complex system with relative ease—your native language! Someone spoke to you, interacted with you, and engaged you in so many games, activities, and discoveries—imaginary and real—which is how you acquired your mother tongue. How can we bring vibrant, language- and activity-rich learning opportunities into every classroom for ELs to develop their new language and literacy skills as their English-speaking peers also expand their academic language?

➤ Many English learners leave school at 3:00 pm and will be using their home language for the rest of the day (which is something we fully respect and encourage as one path to multilingualism and a strong cultural identity). Yet, if interacting in English is limited to the school hours, how can we make sure that time is maximized?

➤ On average, secondary teachers were found to talk up to 70 percent or more of class time (Goodlad, 2004). The general research on "teacher talk" and the question of how much is too much goes back to the 1960s and 1970s. Fifty years later, educators understand that students—especially English learners—need multiple opportunities to exchange thoughts and ideas in a school setting. How much time in a given day is devoted to supporting ELs in expressing their learning?

➤ We have found that some students (both native-English speaking and English learners alike) struggle to write in the academic voice expected in schools. How can ELs learn to write well in a new language and express themselves logically and clearly in writing if they have not had sufficient opportunities to practice what they would write about by discussing it first with others?

So why is the implementation of small groups and partner work not the default model used by teachers? Teachers we work with offer several reasons: lack of classroom space; length of time and effort it takes to rearrange groups and (possibly) desks; the seemingly chaotic, noisy learning environment; the amount of material to be covered; and children may not get along. Do any of these classroom issues sound familiar to you? Teachers have also reported that some parents do not want their youngsters working in teams with ELs because they feel it will slow down their children's progress. In addition, students sometimes complain they are uncomfortable in teams when non-English speakers revert to their native language with one another because they do not understand what ELs are saying.

These concerns need not hold you back because research clearly shows that collaborative learning strategies—whether small group or partners—maximize student engagement and student learning.

RESEARCH TO WATCH

➤ Zhang, Niu, Munawar, and Anderson (2016) examined proficient discussion groups and the influence of teacher talk and student backgrounds. They found that "productive discussions occur when students hold the floor for an extended period and have interpretive authority and control of turn taking" (p. 203). This study supports previous research that reflects similar findings for English-speaking populations. The takeaway is that effective scaffolding and modeling for peer discussion groups are successful strategies to pursue for small groups as ways to facilitate language-learning opportunities.

➤ Zwiers (2014) explained that in small groups, students can learn to listen and use "connective phrases" (p. 159), which helps to develop the skills of communication and respect. Examples of academic language that can be modeled in small groups are: I respectfully agree; I would like to build on that point by adding _____; However, one question I still have is _____; I can add to the discussion with this key point about: _____.

➤ Hattie (2012) found that students who have opportunities to interact with their peers and demonstrate support for each other had positive outcomes for both academic learning and socialization.

➤ Gibbons (2015) placed a special emphasis on what she referred to as "literate talk," which "serves as a bridge between activity-related talk and more formal written registers of subject learning" (p. 83).

➤ Short (2018) reminded teachers that students can often "benefit from a few moments of quiet before speaking" (para. 3). Such time, which she refers to as "silent seconds," is a way for students to transition their thoughts from thinking to speaking, as it builds confidence to speak with peers.

🔑 SOME KEY TERMS

While most of the terms we use in this chapter are commonly shared by educators across all classrooms, some might be new or used differently here. For the sake of clarity, here are descriptions for the most common terms you may come across in the literature about grouping for English learners:

➤ *Cooperative learning.* The organization of classroom activities that enhance the linguistic, academic, and social experiences of the learners.

➤ *Group work.* Three or more students collaborating to respond to a challenge.

➤ *Language communities.* The way groups use words, symbols, and expressions (Facione & Gittens, 2016).

➤ *Pair work.* Two students collaborating to solve a problem.

➤ *SWIRL.* An emerging acronym for an integrated classroom practice of students *S*peaking, *W*riting, *I*nteracting, *R*eading, and *L*istening.

UNPACKING THE COMMON FRAMEWORK

Using the common framework established for this book, let's see what successful student teams do to support each other's learning:

➤ *Common Purpose.* When students are grouped together, ensure that they work toward a common academic and literacy goal rather than sitting side-by-side attending to their own assignment. Try this:

> ➢ Establish clear goals that may be created by the teacher, by the students, or by the teacher and students.

➤ Ensure clarity of those goals—including both language and content targets (Hattie, 2012); remember that learning happens through positive social interactions.

➤ Devise ways for the students to develop ownership of their learning.

➤ Verify that the students can articulate the goals to their peers, their teachers, and their parents.

➤ *Shared Mindset.* Simply assigning students to groups will not forge a collaborative approach to learning. Students must want to work together—they must develop a shared ownership of the task and believe that together they can do better on the target tasks than they would alone.

➤ *Build team spirit.* The group should celebrate the opportunity to work together. You can encourage team spirit by giving a few minutes of time at the beginning of a project/assignment for the team to chat and build rapport.

➤ *Offer choices.* When you offer choices within the group arrangements, students feel as though they have more ownership of their learning. For instance, ask the students whether they would rather create an iMovie or develop a skit as a summative assessment.

➤ *Create a shared vision.* Give students an opportunity to decide what they will be creating and how they will go about it.

➤ *Stop and check.* The group must stay focused on whether they are keeping the task or learning target in mind. Frequent "stop and checks" or keeping your "eyes on the prize" are ways for students to develop self-regulation skills while building rapport and using group processes.

➤ *Diverse Team Membership.* While homogenous grouping allows for targeted interventions, group diversity builds mutual respect and interdependence. Forming diverse groups may be achieved in several ways:

> ➢ *Flexible grouping.* Groups may be intentionally assigned by the students' levels of language proficiency (Kendall, 2006) or mixed to combine varied levels of language proficiency. Additionally, English learners and their English-speaking peers can be organized into flexible groups based on the assignment or the needs of the students.

> ➢ *Interest- or topic-based groups.* Such groupings do not consider language proficiency levels but rather allow students to choose the topic of interest to which they are best aligned. Groups formulated on interest rather than language ability have the inherent benefit of the students' motivation.

> ➢ *Outcome-based grouping.* In this type of small-class grouping, students choose the product in which they are most interested. Tomlinson (2001, 2003) developed this concept for differentiation of instruction. Students who are encouraged to choose the final product will most likely work harder toward their goal. For instance, students can choose between writing a play, writing a report, creating an iMovie, or conducting an interview. Although each group may, for example, be studying the Holocaust, each will showcase their learning targets through different means.

➤ *Supportive Environment.* While some student groups will thrive if left to their own devices, others will languish. While at times the best choice is to allow students to figure out a problem and protocol on their own, groups often do better if appropriate supports are in place. How can you accomplish this? Here are some suggestions:

> ➤ Establish and practice routines for starting and ending group work.
> ➤ Create structures and protocols that support student learning and value student input.
> ➤ Offer a range of visual, graphic, linguistic, and interactive scaffolds.
> ➤ Allow extra time for students to change their timelines or make modifications to their work.

We can hear you asking, "How about teaching some new content, or modeling some new skills, or even reading aloud to the class?" We agree that minilessons, teacher demonstrations, and hands-on learning are essential in every class. The challenge is to increase the type of instructional delivery that engages students and, thereby, optimizes ELs' learning. What English learners need is very similar to what all students need (Goldenberg & Coleman, 2010): a safe, supportive environment in which learning is meaningful and engaging; fear of failure is diminished because risk taking and exploration are the norm; and language is used purposefully and through multiple modalities. The most significant difference is that ELs have two (or sometimes more) languages to figure out and respond to what is going on in the classroom and beyond. To that end, make sure all languages spoken by the students in the classroom are honored as tools of communication through multilingual signs, anchor charts, dictionaries, electronic devices used as resources, and peer bridges (students who speak the same native language interacting with each other for peer support and meaning making).

⏱ QUICK TIP 1: WATCH OUT FOR THE SILENT PERIOD!

Watch out for the silent period—a time when ELs may have not yet communicated. Don't force students to speak but recognize that the mind is never silent. English learners in this preproduction phase are receptive learners and great communicators in their native language or via using alternate modalities. They are beginning to process the language that they hear in this initial stage of exposure. While this phase can generally last for a few months, depending on each student's comfort level, it can be shorter or longer.

Expect individual language variances and remember what Ohta (2001) cautions about: "[The] seemingly silent learner is neither passive nor disengaged but is involved in an intrapersonal interactive process" (p. 12). Meanwhile, support native language expression and multimodal ways of learning and communicating that honors learners' private speech (internal thoughts and silent participation in learning).

USING TEAMS IN A SWIRL-ING CLASSROOM THAT ENGAGES AND SUPPORTS ELs

The concept of SWIRL-ing classrooms has come up in several prominent publications without identifying a definite source of origin. We believe it is an example of shared understanding and thinking alike, independent of each other, to recognize the importance of integrating the four language domains and shifting the order from listening, speaking, reading, and writing to speaking, writing, reading, and listening (Dodge & Honigsfeld, 2014). We have come across the idea of SWIRL in several blog posts (Burkins & Yaris, 2013; Cooper, 2012) that emphasized the need to ensure active engagement with language and literacy tasks. The acronym is sometimes interpreted as Speak, Write, Interact, Read, and Listen, emphasizing the need to practice productive language skills and build communicative competence rather than merely expecting students to learn English by practicing grammatical structures (Cooper, 2012). Fernandez Anderson (2015) suggests that "language components are interrelated following a format of SWIRL (speaking and writing integrated with reading and listening) that give opportunity for social and academic language development in a holistic and meaningful way" (p. 73).

Why is SWIRL-ing so important for ELs? All students, especially language learners, need time to work with and through complex academic language to be successful in any content area. We believe it to be a cornerstone of effective EL instruction to offer a variety of opportunities for students to grapple with new content through authentic speaking, writing, interacting, reading, and listening—SWIRL-ing—activities. It is important to remember that although ELs may not be fluent in English, they are often capable of grade-level academic work and should be given every opportunity to interact with each other and their native English-speaking peers.

HOW TO SWIRL

Imagine that you begin each day by setting an intention to create a SWIRL-ing classroom that addresses the language and literacy challenges of all learners while ensuring high levels of engagement and collaboration. It is no small feat! One powerful way to achieve this is to intentionally build a language community within a text-rich environment that is sizzling with opportunities for speaking, writing, interacting, reading, and listening. Figure 2.2 presents examples of rich choices to meaningfully integrate the four language domains—speaking, writing, reading, listening—into every lesson.

Ways to Integrate the Four Language Domains into Every Lesson   FIGURE 2.2

Speaking	Writing	Reading	Listening
• Agree/disagree	• Ask/answer	• Discover	• Act out
• Answer/ask	questions	• Distinguish	• Arrange
questions	• Brainstorm	• Explore	• Distinguish
• Compare	• Classify	• Find	• Categorize
• Converse	• Collect	• Find specific	• Choose
• Debate	• Compare/	information	• Follow
• Define	contrast	• Identify	directions
• Describe	• Create	• Infer	• Identify
• Discuss	• Describe	• Interpret	• Indicate
• Explain	• Edit	• Locate	• Label
• Express	• Evaluate	• Make	• Listen
• Give instruc-	• Explain	connections	• Match
tions	• Illustrate	• Match	• Order
• Identify	• Journal	• Preview	• Point
• Name	• Label	• Predict	• Recognize
• Predict	• List	• Read silently	• Role-play
• Pronounce	• Order/organize	• Read aloud	• Select
• Rehearse	• Record	• Skim	• Show
• Repeat	• Revise		• Sort
• Rephrase	• State and		• Tell
• Respond	justify		
• Restate	• Offer an		
• Share	opinion		
• Summarize	• Summarize		
• Tell	• Support		
• Use	• Write/take		
vocabulary	notes		

SEE IT IN ACTION

You might be wondering how to successfully integrate all four language skills and also ensure student–to–student interaction. One effective strategy, called an anticipation guide—sometimes referred to as an anticipatory set—may serve multiple purposes in the SWIRL-ing classroom. First and foremost, it will be an effective tool for you to activate your students' prior knowledge or validate ELs' existing understandings. Anticipation guides also allow students to preview an upcoming lesson by reading a series of statements that are either true or false. Learning is not a linear process. Multiple meaningful exposures to the content are needed. Dodge and Honigsfeld (2014) note that anticipation guides address the following three aspects of working with background knowledge and help scaffold learning in multiple ways:

➤ They *assess* prior knowledge by having students evaluate a teacher-provided list of statements about the topic.

➤ They *activate* what students already know and make apparent the misconceptions that some students hold.

➤ They *build* background in several ways: they preview key concepts and introduce vocabulary prior to reading; they provide a purpose for reading; and they help students integrate and consolidate new learnings (p. 22).

Figure 2.3 is a template that includes teacher-provided statements connected to an inquiry-based science lesson for an elementary class. In the classic practice, anticipation guides invite students to *read* each statement (alone or in pairs) prior to having access to the entire text and decide whether they agree or disagree with those statements. They can *write* down some notes in the margins for further discussion. Next, they can engage in a paired or small-group discussion to compare their notions about the topic and *speak* about how they came up with arguments for or against a statement and to *listen* to divergent points of view.

Next, the students may *listen* to the teacher read a selection aloud, *view* an instructional video, or *read* the assigned or self-selected text. In our example, students *participate* in a hands-on exploration or project-based learning (discussed in detail in Chapter 3). They can continue to write notes or engage in guided or small-group discussions as the lesson unfolds. The statements are revisited after the lesson, when students have an opportunity to reassess the same statements. As they may or may not continue to agree or disagree with the statements based on the new information gained from the learning experience, they will have the time to discuss the outcomes of their anticipation guide self-assessment or write a summary statement about what they have learned. ELs will benefit from sentence frames such as these: I used to believe _____ but now I know _____ because _____.

An Anticipation Guide Template for Life Cycles		FIGURE 2.3
Before Reading (Agree or Disagree?)	**Statements**	**After Reading** (Agree or Disagree?)
	1. Does a butterfly have a life cycle?	
	2. Does a cat have a life cycle?	
	3. Does a lilac bush have a life cycle?	
	4. Does a pencil have a life cycle?	
	5. Does a frog have a life cycle?	

Summary Statement 1: Explain your thinking and develop a reason why you think the butterfly, cat, lilac bush, pencil, or frog have life cycles.

Summary Statement 2: (After the inquiry-based lesson), go back to your list and decide if your reason was correct or incorrect. Explain why. Has your thinking changed? If so, how?

⏱ QUICK TIP 2

While the SWIRL-ing acronym serves a key purpose to remind you about integrating the domains and to include interaction among students, there is no strict order in which students can speak, read, listen, and write. Based on ELs' language proficiency, listening might come first in some activities, or reading may proceed writing. SWIRL is a mnemonic device to keep language motion in mind!

SMALL-GROUP COLLABORATIONS

Within the small-group context, students will have multiple, close-up opportunities to interact with the material and one another. When working in small groups, student discussions may wander away from their learning goals and become overly social. You may have often wondered how you can ensure that your students are on task and remain productive while working in small groups, especially if there are some language barriers. It is helpful to offer English learners outlines of what they need to accomplish or key points to talk about during group work. A checklist or partially completed outline will further scaffold student learning and help them remain on task. See Figure 2.4 for a sample checklist that invites students to individually reflect on their participation (and place check marks in the appropriate boxes).

Strategies to make the small-group work productive. For more productive small-group work, consider the following:

➤ *Group norms.* Jointly create an anchor chart that states what the group expectations are and how to self-assess and reflect on one's participation. Students need to be able to define and then monitor their own participation.

Student Participation Reflection Checklist	Judy	Aafreen	Jose	Kelli
Did you explain the assignment to each other?				
Did you decide who will be the recorder of the notes?				
Did you participate and share your own point of view?				
Was your point of view changed after talking with your peers?				
What questions do you still have about the main idea and the characters' actions?				

FIGURE 2.4

➤ *Resources.* Provide multilingual, multimodal materials and technology resources to facilitate meaningful interaction among all students. Electronic dictionaries, Google translate, and multilingual or multilevel versions of the same text are all helpful in this regard.

➤ *Routines and structures.* Make sure students know what to expect when working in groups. As suggested previously, checklists, visual clues, and posters work well here as reminders. Most ELs thrive in a structured learning environment; it offers them safety.

➤ *Examples.* Model or role-play the type of interaction you are looking to see within groups. English learners appreciate when activities are predictable, and they will become more interactive and productive when clear examples are given. Think of various ways to *show* rather than *tell* what your expectations are.

➤ *Accountability.* Consider how students working in teams might provide opportunities to assess small-group work. Some teachers circulate the room to observe student talk, to ask questions, and to document progress by jotting down anecdotal notes. Other teachers require all students in the small group to complete pencil-and-paper tasks individually in collaboration with their teams and randomly select one of the students' papers as an assessment for the team's work. In this way, all team members are invested in every member's understanding and being on task.

➤ *Practice, practice, practice.* Students will get better!

Strategic grouping to make small-group work productive. There are many ways to change the grouping arrangements of the classroom by moving students rather than moving furniture. Here are some of the most popular and productive arrangements:

➤ *Jigsaw.* This is a grouping strategy that works for all grade levels and language proficiencies, as it develops both communication skills and teamwork. In a jigsaw, students are like pieces of a puzzle. Members of the class are organized into groups—generally by the teacher—and work on a shared assignment. After each piece of the jigsaw is completed, students may present what they have learned. The groups can also be rearranged into new groups to extend and share their learning with their classmates.

➤ *Expert jigsaw group* (Thousand, Villa, & Nevin, 2015). Students research and develop their materials individually and then join a small group based on areas of investigation or research. The teams can then share ideas and information and plan ways to teach the content. The small group may then present to other groups or the individuals can return to their original groups and present their new knowledge. In one classroom we supported, 4th graders studied Native American tribes in a jigsaw arrangement. Each group was responsible for researching a different tribe and creatively presenting their findings. As a culminating activity, parents and other members of the local community were invited to hear the students' presentations.

➤ *Carousel.* This can be a culminating activity after individual students or small groups complete their work. The finished product is then displayed, and students can walk around the room and ask questions or offer feedback—perhaps on sticky notes. The benefit of the carousel approach is that students get to see the other groups' work without necessarily listening to oral presentations. Students can read about the projects at their own pace. Make sure you leave space between the projects or presentations and start different groups at different points on the carousel to avoid crowding. Some teachers like to use timers to help the children move about the carousel in a more organized way.

Regardless of the small grouping arrangement you try, the benefits to English learners are clear: enhanced opportunities for collaboration, practice time for SWIRL-ing communication, students learning from and with one another, out-of-seat stretches while moving around the classroom, and a relaxed learning environment.

⏱ QUICK TIP 3: GO TO THE CONVERSATIONS!

Move around the room and listen to small-group discussions for 30 seconds to a minute while keeping the groups on task. Look for outward indicators of productive group learning (such as body language and movement associated with meaningful conversations), and shared visual gaze on materials. Probe or prompt students if needed but move on to nurture group process and independence.

PARTNER WORK

What are the pitfalls to avoid when pairing students? They may simply be working side by side, without any intentional or focused shared learning. To ensure quality partner work—which truly reflects the contributions of two students—strategies for working together should be modeled by teachers and by other students. Consider the following strategies to make partner work productive:

➤ *Pairing with a language partner.* When you have beginners (also referred to as entering or Level 1 students), take advantage of the tremendous knowledge and skills they already have and allow them to process information in their native tongue with their language partners (provided you have more than one child speaking a particular language).

➤ *Reading and writing buddies.* For peer-tutoring purposes, create partnerships that include English-speaking and EL students, both of whom will benefit—ELs will benefit from receiving the peer modeling and English-speaking students will benefit from increased opportunities for reading and writing with feedback.

➤ *Learning criteria.* Be sure to have a set of pre-established criteria, or Look Fors, so that you can give students meaningful feedback on their participation in the group discussions. Better yet, establish those criteria with your students to help develop ownership of their learning and participation.

➤ *Different partners for different purposes.* Establish different student partnerships for classroom routines and for core-content activities.

➤ *Learning on your feet.* Get your students out of their seats for brain breaks, as well as to have them mix and mingle while music is playing (Kagan & Kagan, 2009).

Frequently used learning activities that support peer-to-peer interaction include

➤ *Turn and Talk*. We challenge you to avoid asking questions directed to the entire class and then calling on a single student. Instead, have students turn to a partner and briefly share some ideas before you invite students to offer a response to a reading or a question in front of a larger group.

➤ *Think-Pair-Share*. Soto (2014) suggested that Think-Pair-Share is one of the most basic yet impactful strategies to enhance ELs' academic oral language development. Students are invited to individually read a selection or reflect on a question posed by the teacher, then pair up and share their ideas.

➤ *Partner Read/Write*. This is a structured paired activity that promotes reading and writing time. Reading or writing "buddies" are grouped together based on similar reading or writing levels. This activity can be used several times during a week, and students have opportunities to "check in" with each other for chapter reading or writing an end to a story. You can support partner groups' level of independence by providing them with anticipation guides or questions to answer after reading several paragraphs to the end of a chapter. This independent activity works best when students use close reading strategies and shared writing to demonstrate comprehension of the material. For an extended partner read/write, you can have a group share at the end of the assignment.

➤ *Line Up and Fold* (Kagan & Kagan, 2009). For another way for students to engage in active conversation and discussion on their feet, first have students line up in a particular order (by birthday or alphabetically). Once students have formed a straight line, direct the first student at one end of the line to walk down to face the last student at the other end of the line, followed by the other students until the line is "folded in half" and everyone has a partner.

➤ *Phone a Friend*. This strategy may remind you of a "helpline." In this simple idea, if a student cannot generate an answer or is stuck on a concept, they can phone (ask) a friend for help.

Instead of saying, "I don't know," being able to phone a friend allows all students an opportunity to ask for help.

➤ *Inside-Outside Circle.* Organize two groups of students with an equal number in both groups. The students form concentric circles as the outside circle faces inward and the inside circle faces outward. The teacher poses a question, and the students share with their partners (Kagan, Kagan, & Kagan, 2016).

➤ *Minipresentations.* Students work independently to research a given topic or self-selected topic and then make a presentation to a small group whose topics are somehow connected. For instance, the student who is learning about elephants may connect with a student who is studying giraffes and a student who is learning about Africa. Drawing a diagram to show the interconnectedness of topics helps children see relationships and commonalities in their research.

IN CONVERSATION WITH TEACHERS

We asked educators around the country the following question: How do you ensure that ELs are fully included in the classroom? And how do you know you have a SWIRL-ing classroom? Here are three answers we received. As you read them, consider how they can help inform your practice.

Katherine Neumair and Greg Sill, a Smithtown, New York, high school co-teaching team, shared a recent example of their collaborative approach to teaching an integrated high school class where ELs learn alongside their English-speaking peers:

> *As co-teachers of an integrated high school social studies course, we intentionally employ strategies that support all students' academic language and literacy development. Here is a recent example from our class. Over the course of three days, we have been teaching our*

students the various economic systems that can be found in government. On day one, we taught the students about capitalism and utilitarianism by using Nearpod. We used the I SEE graphic organizer to help students review what they know (this is a four-step activity designed to unpack a complex concept by illustrating it, stating what it is, elaborating on the brief definition, and giving examples). In our classroom, students are currently organized into groups of six; three students sit in the front row of their grouping and three in the back row. Within each group, we asked the students in the front row to focus on capitalism while the back row would focus on utilitarianism. As we walked students through the graphic organizer, we modeled on the board what information we were looking for. Starting with "I," we asked students to illustrate or draw a picture that would show their assigned economic system. First, the students had to write when they created their definition and their examples. They were also asked to do some reading in order to create these definitions, enabling them to review their notes. Next, the students interacted with one another when the front row and the back row were asked to share their information and teach one another about their assigned economic system. Finally, students listened to one another through this interaction. Using the graphic organizer allowed us to SWIRL with our students. Students needed to speak to one another not only when they were first creating the I SEE for their economic system, but also when we asked the whole group to share their work with one another.

Jackie Griffin, language development coach, Country Meadows Elementary, Kildeer School, District 96, shared how Thinking Maps and Kagan Cooperative Structures engage her students and ensure active learning opportunities:

Thinking Maps (Buckner, 2009) and Kagan Structures (Kagan & Kagan, 2015) are a part of my co-taught classes every day. We use multiple maps throughout the day in every subject as tools for students to organize their thoughts. Some of our favorite maps to use are Circle Maps, Tree Maps, and Multiflow Maps. A Circle Map is used when you are brainstorming about an idea. It can be one circle or you can divide it into sections to organize your thoughts. A Tree Map is to categorize information as well as give examples or definitions of the category. A Multiflow Map is used to show a cause-and-effect sequence. When I learned cause and effect, there were just two events—one is the cause and one is the effect. We love the multiflow because you start with an event in the middle, then you think of what caused the event and, finally, what happened as a result. It is a three-part series instead of just two. We love using the Multiflow Map to have students reflect on their own behavior. They think about their actions, what caused them to behave in a certain way, and how it affected other people. Each map is used for a certain thought process. Our entire school uses the eight maps, so when a teacher sees the students on day one of school and says, "Let's brainstorm about how we want our class to operate," all of the students would know to draw a circle map because they have been practicing using that tool each and every year for the same thought process of brainstorming.

Last week, my 2nd graders used multiple maps while planning and writing a narrative story. To begin, students had some personal think time to brainstorm ideas for their story. All the students drew a divided circle map in order to brainstorm the characters, setting, problem, and solution to their story. After a few minutes, the students did a Su, Hu, Pu (Stand Up, Hand Up, Pair Up) to find a writing buddy. The buddies then shared their story ideas with each other using a timed pair share to ensure that each person had equal participation and individual accountability. The students gave feedback to each other by giving One Glow and One Grow to each other to tell one thing they did well and one thing that would make their story better. The students then went back to their seats to add anything they heard and liked from their partner. The next step in the writing process is to plan. The thought process for planning is putting events in sequential order, so the students use a Flow Map. A Flow Map in our classroom is at least 3 boxes (or events) to signal a beginning, a middle, and an end. If the students choose to do a Flow Map, they draw a Flow Map and add character thoughts, feelings, and actions underneath their event box. This helps the students remember to add those details in their story when they write it. After each step of the writing process, the students partner up with their writing buddy and share their thoughts and give feedback. This helps when it is time to edit and revise because the partner already knows the story. Throughout this writing process, students are practicing many skills: speaking, writing, reading, listening, providing feedback, interacting with other students, and peer editing. We choose to strategically pair our students based on writing level or language level in order to strategically intervene with students. Our students are willing to work cooperatively and learn from each other not only through the writing process but in all activities because Kagan Structures have helped build social skills, peer interactions, and self-confidence.

Winnie Yang, ESOL teacher (formerly 2nd grade teacher) at Sudley Elementary School, Prince William County Public Schools, Manassas, Virginia, describes how she creates lessons for the study of words within an open-class environment:

I have a 4th grade class—many of my students are Spanish-speaking ELLs—and I work in collaboration with Mrs. Miller, the language arts teacher. Students in the class are split into different reading groups, and Mrs. Miller meets with them throughout the week to work on reading comprehension strategies. Within these learning groups, students can interact with each other and discuss the work they are completing. Sometimes students are able to work together to practice the reading and recording of questions for a specific skill (e.g., identifying nonfiction text structures). Other times this is word study, in which they manipulate and work with the focus Greek and Latin roots for the week. These groups are structured so that students move throughout the room during the language arts period; students don't have an assigned seat but rather an area that they congregate in when rotating through a specific "station." This allows for movement throughout the block and establishes an atmosphere of collaboration among students.

I often spend time with students who are working on word study, which in 4th grade consists of understanding Greek and Latin roots and applying them to their reading comprehension and writing. Whenever possible, I try to connect unknown words and roots back to the students' home language (of Spanish) as a form of a mnemonic device. Students recently worked with numeric prefixes (e.g., uni-, bi-, tri-, etc.) and practiced segmenting multisyllabic words to determine the meaning of those words with affixes. For some of the root words, I like to pull in cognates from Spanish to help students remember meanings, such as how "annual" in "biannual" sounds like "año" (year) in Spanish, or how "lingual" in "bilingual" sounds like "lengua" (tongue/language) in Spanish. I also discuss with the students how people say someone can speak many tongues, or languages. By introducing the idea of connecting unknown words in English to familiar words in the students' native languages, they begin to think of other ways the two languages can be connected to support learning.

⏱ QUICK TIP 4: USE MULTIPLE LANGUAGES!

Do you wonder if it is appropriate for students to speak to their partner in their native language or even to "mix" languages? The answer is yes! Students may use their native language as a bridge to understand the new content they are learning for the first time. If a student has prior knowledge about a topic, it is an asset-based strategy to activate their prior knowledge, be it in their L1, L2, or possibly even their L3. It is helpful for English learners to build on the literacy they have achieved in their native language whenever possible.

THE ROLE OF THE TEACHER AFTER TEAMS ARE CREATED IN THE CLASSROOM

Teachers perceive their roles in different ways when creating teams or cooperative groups in the classroom. How do you perceive your role as you promote flexible grouping? Are you a facilitator who walks around and listens? Are you a hands-on participant who spends a minute or two in each group taking on the role of the student? Are you an observer or a notetaker? Do you direct traffic and the flow of conversation in small groups or for partners?

There is no one way to foster classroom discourse or cooperative grouping. If you answered Yes to any of these questions, you may be the teacher who changes roles as often as the grouping changes. When forming cooperative learning groups, ELs could be assigned specific roles aligned to their abilities, such as artist, recorder, or speaker. This way, students are active rather than passive participants. In short, you may organize groups and vary their roles often, but you need to respect the student-centeredness of small groups and should not step in to direct the interactions, student exchanges, or ideas that are emerging from the teams.

🧰 TECH TOOLBOX

Make use of technology tools and online resources that support building collaborative classroom learning environments.

GOOGLE CLASSROOM

Within the Google Classroom, students collaborate using tools such as Google docs and slides as they collaboratively research topics, share their learning, and prepare reports and presentations.

FLUENTU

Laughing at funny videos with your friends? Practicing your sentences? FluentU is an app that students can have on their tablets or a website that they can access from their computers. The video-driven technology tool offers an individualized learning experience in which a child's new vocabulary and learned vocabulary are tracked. Visit https://www.fluentu.com/blog/english/best-apps-learning-english-esl-students/.

GREEN SCREEN BY DO INK

This app allows students to combine green screen video technology with photography, artwork, and research. Students enjoy telling their story, creatively expressing themselves, and sharing what they have to say. Visit http://www.doink.com/description/.

CONCLUSION

Students must speak to students. They need to have opportunities to interact with each other, and the complex material we present to them, in authentic, engaging ways. When they do so, language becomes the most essential tool at their disposal— they must use it! In a student-centered classroom, the students are doing most of the talking and processing, while their language development is fully supported through writing, reading, and listening.

In the next chapter, we further challenge you to relinquish control, enter into a learning partnership with your students, and shift your instructional role to that of a master facilitator. You will be in full support of your students to engage in academic discoveries through problem solving as well as inquiry- and project-based learnings that require teamwork. And the ultimate gain? Your students develop ownership of their own learning experiences.

Taking It Further: Reflection Questions

1. What are the most compelling reasons for taking a team approach to creating a more inclusive, culturally responsive and sustaining, and linguistically vibrant classroom community?
2. In what ways has the concept of a SWIRL-ing classroom affirmed what you have been doing in your classroom?
3. What are the greatest challenges you anticipate or might have already faced when shifting from a teacher-centered instructional modality to a student-centered one? How did you overcome those challenges?

Additional Resources

Do you see what others see? *The New York Times* offers a Learning Network's series entitled *What's Going On in this Picture?* You can ask students to look carefully at the image that has been stripped of its caption. Students can describe what they think the picture is about or predict what they think is happening. Visit https://www.nytimes.com/column /learning-whats-going-on-in-this-picture.

Are you familiar with Nanowrimo? National Novel Writing Month takes place in November and challenges students to write a novel in 30 days! The Young Writers Program supports K–12 students and educators as they pursue their writing dreams. Visit https://ywp.nanowrimo.org/.

Do you want to help your students grow successfully? The Search Institute has produced the Developmental Relationships Framework with five key elements that can enhance relationships—express care, challenge growth, provide support, share power, and expand possibilities. The 20 specific actions can be introduced to students and offer positive examples and encouraging language in an easy-to-read chart. Visit https://www.search-institute.org/developmental-relationships /developmental-relationships-framework/.

CHAPTER 3

TEACHERS AND STUDENTS ON THE SAME TEAM

[S]he asked students to get in their groups once again, analyze the next chapter using the same questions, and come up with questions of their own.

The bell rang, and Renata Kim drew her students' attention to the novel they had been reading, To Kill a Mockingbird. *The previous week, the class had completed an analysis of one of the chapters and Ms. Kim chose to review that chapter by not only sharing her own curiosity about the reading but also by crafting questions she had about the chapter that still remained.*

Ms. Kim reintroduced part of the plot—how people all over the surrounding area came to the town of Maycomb to watch the trial. She recounted some of the descriptions of the characters as they headed into town, and she wondered aloud how the townspeople might have felt about all those visitors jamming up their streets. Ms. Kim recalled for her students with great detail the first time she visited a large city as a child and how overwhelmed she had felt. She also shared a few other lingering questions that she had.

Ms. Kim then asked students if they had any questions about the chapter that still persisted with them: Was there anything about the chapter that may have astonished you or engaged your thinking in some way that led to you having more questions about the text? Can you relate part of the text to your own experiences? She gave students a few moments to look back at the chapter, and then she had them turn and talk in small groups to share the questions and connections they had made with the reading that they hadn't shared with each other before. Ms. Kim then solicited responses from the student groups. The questions students shared and how they personally related to the content sparked a few brief discussions. Subsequently, she asked students to get in their groups once again, analyze the next chapter using the same questions, and generate questions of their own.

We all agree that one of the primary purposes of schooling is to ensure that our students become independent learners and critical thinkers. Additionally, when students grow up, they need skills that serve them as they become part of adult working teams and communities. Having teachers and students conferring on the same team with the same goals is one way to ensure that we become facilitators and coaches for our students so that they may step up and take responsibility for their own learning.

In this chapter, we address the four core principles of teamwork and show how common purpose, shared mindset, diverse team membership, and supportive environment contribute to successful partnerships between students and teachers. This chapter also discusses how to shift instructional roles so that

English learners make the most of their time in school through quality teacher–student collaboration. Think about such partnerships as pathways for language and literacy development in the Vygotskyan tradition: learning happens best in the presence and under the guidance of a knowledgeable other! For this reason, we believe that carefully crafted opportunities for engagement and shared exploration create teacher–student partnerships in which students develop ownership of their own learning. With this in mind, we examine ways to foster inquiry- and project-based models of instruction as well as independent learning.

WHY PARTNER WITH STUDENTS?

A co-designed partnership between students and teachers might be a novel idea for some. Did it strike you as such? For many others, it might be a well-established, everyday practice. Have you ever taken the time to discuss with students the need for building a partnership and how to do so? There are many compelling reasons to encourage teacher–student collaborations, and we will outline a few of them.

CONSIDER THIS

Working in collaboration has been found to be transformative:

➤ When students at any grade level engage in project-based learning over their school years, there is an "accumulating effect" (Larmer, 2016; Larmer, Mergendoller, & Boss, 2015) of building new knowledge and skills. As a result, they will be more likely to contribute ideas and their talents when presented with authentic problems—in classrooms or the working world.

➤ Collaboration builds trust. These might seem like three simple words but a difficult concept. What can we accomplish without trust and relationship? Levine (2016) explains that a "stable democratic system depends on civic relationships," (p. 33) and so the classroom is a microcosm of society in which we can build trust—trust between and among students, teachers, and community members. Let's begin with recognizing that teachers and students are on the same team!

➤ There seem to be ever-growing challenges that the next generations face, be it social, political, economic, scientific, medical, and others. Teachers can no longer be considered the holders of all knowledge. We are not! We need to recognize the capacity and the original thinking that the next generation can bring to these societal challenges. Let's embrace the opportunity to build partnerships with youth as a stepping-stone to prepare them for taking action later on.

➤ In the adult world of corporations, bureaucracies, and industries, students will face challenges and will be asked to brainstorm and problem solve. How can we lead the charge to foster collaboration with students that will foster much-needed life skills later in life?

Think about why it is important to collaborate across various contexts and consider the processes that foster teacher–student collaborative practices. Teachers can model collaboration, especially in co-taught classrooms (Dove & Honigsfeld, 2018), through sharing responsibilities, modeling problem solving, and professional verbal exchanges. Visualize the power of two teachers role-playing collaborative conversations with an emphasis on shared ownership of the problem, academic language use, active listening, and creative co-construction of solutions. If there is only one teacher in the classroom, there are many ways you can also model collaborative practices and team building through teacher-talk with flexible groups of students. You can model one-on-one dialogues, small-group debates, or even speeches in large groups by showing how to respectfully engage others while also inviting differences of opinions.

Do you have clear goals as your teacher–student partnerships are designed? Do you intentionally model the appropriate paths for problem solving with your ELs as well as the formal language needed to communicate in an academic voice? Jensen (2013) posits that many teachers "avoid explicit teaching in problem solving" (p. 58). He suggests that teachers model and scaffold the problem-solving process as well as "teach transferable models for problem solving" (p. 59). In the type of teacher–student partnership we advocate for, teachers are role models who can explain the *thinking* behind the problem solving and break it down into steps. They continuously challenge their students and invite them to contribute, no matter what their language proficiency level is or what language or modality they are using, with the ultimate goal of developing student ownership of the learning process. We have seen in numerous schools and classrooms that amplifying student voice through teaming creates linguistic growth, advocacy, and passion for learning!

RESEARCH TO WATCH

➤ Recent research on the developmental stages of children and adolescents supported by neurobiological breakthroughs shows that the brain changes as children grow. "Studies have shown that stress during the teenage years can have long-lasting effects" (Perkins-Gough, 2015, p. 20). Using MRIs and PET scans to map areas of brain connectivity and circuitry allows scientists and teachers to better understand students' decision-making processes and judgment. Such breakthroughs continue to inform teacher–student collaborations and perhaps change the practices of ability grouping (student self-fulfilling prophesies). Perkins-Gough (2015) reports in an interview with Dr. Frances E. Jensen that IQs—once considered to be innate—can change in the teenage years. What an eye-opening discovery!

➤ Maslow (1999) may have been correct when he concluded that students would not be able to learn if they did not feel safe or if they felt hungry. Yet, researchers commented on Maslow's well-known hierarchy of needs—physiological (food and shelter), safety, belonging/love, esteem, and self-actualization—questioning the commonly seen triangle depiction and considering whether there can be "an end point to personal growth" (Rowan, 1998, para. 19). Others questioned whether there might be true rankings for security. Even though there are criticisms for his theories, much of what Maslow suggested continues to make sense. The takeaway is that students' basic physiological and social-emotional needs must be tended to before learning can take place. From this standpoint, the relationship building between teachers and students must be a priority. Support, nurture, and challenge your students while you take the time to truly understand who they are and whether they feel that they belong. Get to know them and let them get to know you as a trusted role model.

➤ Years of research have pointed to the collective understanding that student-centered classrooms provide many more opportunities for learning and student academic success. The notion of student-centered classrooms may relate back to Dewey (1938), but anecdotes over decades from students as well as teachers support the idea that hands-on, inquiry-based learning directed by students yields engagement and successful school results. "To be successful at challenging new tasks, students need guidance from adults and more experienced peers who can demonstrate what to do and provide models of what success looks like" (Allensworth et al., 2018, p. 10). Make sure your students have access to student-centered classrooms and consider the dynamics between teachers and students that contribute to positive learning environments.

Thinking about the successes and research findings of other educators will help you in your role as teacher, particularly in the building of teacher–student teams. Becoming reflective will help you in knowing what works best for building teams in your classroom! End each day (or even each week) by asking yourself how you connected to your students.

🔑 SOME KEY TERMS

To establish a shared language, we will introduce our definitions of some key concepts that support the notion of teacher–student partnerships.

➤ *Inquiry-based learning.* The foundation of inquiry-based learning rests on the premise that when students are actively engaged in their own learning processes, they will be more successful. This construct requires that the teacher is a guide or facilitator rather than a lecturer and that the students are tackling authentic problem-solving activities.

➤ *Mentoring.* In an enhanced teacher–student relationship, a teacher supports, guides, and encourages individual students in their learning. Mentors may spend extra time with a student to champion academic or career goals and may act as a role model.

➤ *Project-based learning.* Students often communicate and work in small groups or teams conducting activities or research. The projects are student-led, and teachers are facilitators or coaches. At the culmination, projects that showcase students' mastery of the topic are presented to an audience.

➤ *Teacher talk.* Teachers may use this strategy to model academic language that is focused and deliberate. It often allows students to figure out how to generate questions, interact with peers, or complete a problem.

➤ *Translanguaging.* When multilingual learners access their entire linguistic repertoire—rather than communicating in one language at a time—they switch back and forth between two or more linguistic systems.

UNPACKING THE COMMON FRAMEWORK

Utilizing the common framework established for this book, let's see what successful teacher–student teams do to support learning:

➤ *Common Purpose.* When teachers and students forge a partnership in learning, they

> ➢ Build a relationship that fosters communication and interaction.
> ➢ Discuss and establish a shared purpose of learning that will reflect inclusive values of peers, teachers, and parents.
> ➢ Create a shared repertoire (Cox-Petersen, 2011) that reflects routines and structures that teachers and students develop over time.
> ➢ Communicate the common purpose to all stakeholders and speak up on behalf of ELs.

➤ *Shared Mindset.* A shared mindset among teachers and students indicates that they

> ➢ Openly discuss goals, including challenges, hopes, and dreams.
> ➢ Are comfortable asking questions respectfully.
> ➢ Develop a feeling of pride as part of the partnership.

➤ *Diverse Team Membership.* Whether working in a small or large group, the membership of the group should be diverse. The more diverse the group, the more language opportunities and sharing of different ideas are possible. A common mistake when grouping students is to place all the English learners together. This hampers learning and may also diminish access to the new language. There are times that you want to organize students according to their current performance levels and certainly, on occasion, that is an option. However, grouping by ability should be intentional for the instruction of specific content and not used as a strategy to divide students. Teachers can ensure diverse student partnerships are achieved when they

➢ Provide opportunities for students to learn from and share each other's cultural expertise and knowledge.

➢ Organize students so they have opportunities to work with different teachers and benefit from interaction with and mentorship from various perspectives and expertise.

➢ Talk about issues of diversity or even controversial topics such as immigration honestly and openly with their students.

➢ Use icebreakers to group students in varied formations.

➤ *Supportive Environment.* Students report that they perform differently in varied classroom contexts based on their personal level of engagement as well as teacher practices within a classroom environment. Innovative use of school space such as learning labs, makerspace, student commons, and outdoor learning areas may all contribute to creating an environment conducive to creative collaboration. It is important to remember that as the grade level increases, the work becomes more challenging. Therefore, teachers build a supportive environment when they

> ➤ Find out what students need and how they learn best.
> ➤ Employ intentional strategies for student engagement.
> ➤ Implement practices of teacher–student collaboration in the learning process.
> ➤ Create a sense of belonging.
> ➤ Use opportunities to engage other teachers from the school building in activities that compare and contrast points of view and focus on varied cultural experiences.

When we talk about teamwork in this chapter, we focus on the unique relationships between students and their teachers. You can probably recall the teachers who significantly impacted your life. You can reflect on how that person—hopefully in a positive way—helped you to learn about yourself in a way that you never did before.

⏱ QUICK TIP 1: TELL YOUR STORY!

Implementing student-created newsletters is one enjoyable way to put teachers and students on the same team and highlight activities and success stories within the district, school, or individual classroom. Students or parents can send their questions in writing and teachers can answer them in the newsletter, *or* teachers can send their questions in writing and students can answer them! Having students and teachers put themselves in each other's shoes is yet another way to build community and share perspectives. Communication is the key!

SEE IT IN ACTION

In this next section, we unpack ways to support student work in small and large group settings. This is one area that teachers and co-teachers can organize groups to aid in student success while forging *partnerships in learning*. Which types of groups do you tend to use most in your classroom?

PARTNERING WITH LARGE GROUPS

In guided or focus lessons—where you are working with a large group or whole class—you might sometimes feel removed from your students. It may feel as though you are standing in front of the room teaching new information but you do not know who is understanding the information. Try asking your students what they have learned and solicit feedback about your teaching so you know what works best for them.

Keep in mind that in supportive learning environments, learners grow socially as well as academically and that educators have a key role in fostering this growth. For English learners, in addition to considering the social and academic trajectories, you will need to intentionally plan for language integration in all learning objectives. As your students become more sophisticated learners, they begin to internalize the benchmarks of quality schoolwork. For instance, students begin to understand the difference between simple answers and in-depth responses. They begin to see relationships between their assignments and assessments, as well as how to use assessment rubrics to inform their work. Therefore, it is helpful for you to model how to study, how to complete assignments, and how to strive to be lifelong learners. They should always see you as a learner, as a partner in learning, and as an educator. Make sure you shift the culture of the classroom from teacher "versus" students to teacher "with" or "and" students by using terms like *we, us,* and *our*.

To make large-group work productive, consider the following:

➤ *Set clear expectations for participating in large groups, where some students might not have as strong of an opportunity to contribute as in smaller groups.* Remember to provide ELs with a toolkit of linguistic supports that they can use to contribute to academic discussions (G. Oliver, personal communication, April 2, 2019).

➤ *Engage students in large-group activities where they have multiple language opportunities such as debates, one-act plays, and discussions that have shared interaction between teachers and students.* What are the characteristics of teachers that students admire? Which ones have you noticed in your own school? Which characteristics do you have that create a partnership with your students? Wilson and Corbett shared two notable characteristics: "someone who went out of his or her way to provide help" and "someone who provided students with a variety of ways through which to learn" (as cited in Hattie, 2012, p. 159).

➤ *Have students use self-talk to reveal to teachers what they need.* Similarly, use of self-talk by teachers may reveal what they need the students to focus on. Hattie (2012) recognizes self-talk as dimensions of prompting and feedback. For example, when you are reading a book aloud and form a theory about what will happen next, pause and model your thinking aloud. Similarly, invite students to do the same to practice this type of academic self-talk.

➤ *End lessons with exit activities so all students have an opportunity to summarize what they learned, what they enjoyed most about the lesson, or what they still want to learn more about in the days ahead.* Focused exit activities enhance language opportunities for all students in any subject area. A Ticket to Leave or an Exit Card helps students communicate what they have learned or still need to learn, as well as how they feel about the learning experience in the class. Teachers can then keep the feedback for planning future lessons or units of study for the following year.

SMALL-GROUP PRODUCTIVITY

As you likely know and have experienced, the discussions of students, when left to work in small groups, may become unfocused or social. To avoid such an occurrence, first make sure you take time to observe what is happening. Some of the social conversations are essential to team building. Move about the room and listen to small-group discussions for 30 seconds to a minute, and keep the groups focused and dynamic through mentoring and guidance. In a successful and productive independent learning situation, teachers should listen for academic language, literacy skills being utilized, and rigorous content simultaneously (Dove, Honigsfeld, & Cohan, 2014). A productive small group will have *all* students interacting with one another to build upon each other's knowledge. This is a wonderful opportunity for English learners to share their prior knowledge and showcase their academic capital, which may be different than what other students have. Outward indicators of productive group learning include body language and movement associated with meaningful conversations as well as shared visual gaze on materials.

To make small-group work productive, consider the following:

➤ *Encourage students to choose their own roles so they stay on task and take ownership of their learning.* In a small reading group, students may be recorders of new vocabulary, illustrators, prompters of questions, timeline experts, or organizers of summary charts and outlines.

➤ *Design a readers theater in which English learners read from scripts* or plays and have opportunities to develop fluency in both speaking and reading.

➤ *Create writers circles so students gain experience as peer writers and peer reviewers.* Students in small-group writing circles can add on to others' ideas, offer different endings for characters or story plots, and inspire each other to be creative.

➤ *Work in pairs, triads, or foursomes* to debate issues related to current events or history and develop confidence in sharing opinions, perspectives, or different points of view.

➤ *Design artists workshops so that students can draw examples of prior knowledge as they construct new knowledge with their peers.* Use art as the medium for small-group presentations that support conversational and academic language.

➤ *Use multiple types of graphic organizers* to record ideas from small-group discussions and offer students ways to record their interactions.

➤ *Play charades as a small-group strategy* to introduce new words, idioms, or unfamiliar expressions.

➤ *Allow students to communicate with words, written notes or letters, images, emojis, music, pictures, or under-one-minute video messages.* Encourage students to quick-draw or quick-write to share their ideas with the class.

➤ *In every classroom, foster community building led by the teacher, co-teachers, or any aides or assistants.* For example, greet students at the door, ask about their weekend, out-of-school lives, sports, and other nonacademic achievements and offer some personal information about yourself.

➤ *Model behaviors.* As students develop higher-order thinking skills, teachers can model how to engage in persuasive discussions or arguments based on evidence. The ability to share ideas using formal language is one example of how teachers can support their English learners with intentional modeling.

➤ *Use a translanguaging method that allows students to "deploy their full linguistic repertoires"* (Garcia, Ibarra Johnson, & Seltzer, 2017, p. 1) as they leverage their native language in addition to their emerging English language skills. In small- or large-group projects, translanguaging allows students to communicate using all available language resources. This may require agreement in teacher–student partnerships and an understanding about the benefits of translanguaging to support complex academic tasks.

See Figures 3.1a and 3.1b for a group reflection activity that invites students to give feedback on their own learning preference and engagement in a lesson that included recording and organizing

Exit Surveys FIGURE 3.1

a. Exit Survey

b. Exit Survey with Dot Stickers/Feedback

ideas, listening to an audiobook, researching on their own, talking with their peers about the target text, reading independently, and conferencing with the teacher. Figure 3.1a shows the pictorial exit survey that records the students' favorite part of the lesson. Figure 3.1b reveals what the exit survey looks like once students place their dot stickers on the exit survey following the lesson.

In both large and small groups, there are ample opportunities to use teacher-talk to model what you are thinking (metacognition), how to solve a problem, or how to add on to another student's ideas.

INQUIRY-BASED TEACHING: HOW IT BENEFITS ELs

Talk to students and you will find—as we did—that they love inquiry-based formats for learning. Using these formats, students (or teachers) may pose a question or share an objective and students seek to answer that question early in the lesson through an exploration of the topic. For English learners, they have an opportunity to activate and connect their background knowledge to the concept before new information is taught. The value of inquiry-based learning is that it sparks students' natural curiosity and helps them relate to what they already know. In selecting inquiry-based strategies, consider the grade level and proficiency level of the students and the complexity of the content area.

INQUIRY-BASED LEARNING

When students engage in meaningful, deep explorations focused on content-area topics that are well connected to authentic reading and writing tasks, their learning will be more substantial. Inquiry-based learning recognizes that students' curiosity and desire to understand drives learning. Lent (2016) reminds us, "One remarkable characteristic of inquiry is that it is done *by* the individual not *to* the individual, and this active form of learning … is what makes knowledge stick" (p. 104). While inquiry-based learning may be implemented by challenging individual students, when done collaboratively, students benefit from shared learning opportunities and interactions with each other and the material. Banchi and Bell (2008) suggest that there are four levels of inquiry (see Figure 3.2) with incrementally more complex expectations for student independence. Figure 3.2 outlines the four levels of inquiry, their purpose, and a brief summary of what students do and what teachers provide.

⏱ QUICK TIP 2: USE STUDENTS' EXPERIENCES!

When creating inquiry-based teams, focus on the *shared experiences* of your students. Have them keep a running diary or log of their successes to share with you. This is one way to document the group's explorations and recognize accomplishments. You will be able to chronicle the achievements of your English learners

Levels of Inquiry			FIGURE 3.2
Inquiry Type	**Purpose**	**What Students Do**	**What Teachers Provide**
Confirmation Inquiry	To introduce the inquiry process	Confirm experientially what is already known	Questions, procedure, solution
Structured Inquiry	To support a scaffolded inquiry process	Generate explanations for what they find	Questions, procedure
Guided Inquiry	To differentiate the inquiry process	Design the procedure of inquiry and generate explanations	Questions
Open Inquiry	To establish ownership of the inquiry process	Design the question and the method of inquiry and generate explanations	Broad parameters

Adapted from Banchi and Bell, 2008.

by viewing the shared experiences of the team. Check out this example in which a group of 3rd grade students, for their final projects, had to explain how all animals depend on the food-making abilities of green plants to survive.

Day Three

Judy and Juan: Hurricane Sandy hit New York, and the neighborhood marsh was devasted due to the fast influx of saltwater. Kenny: The pond in his backyard in San Salvador was ruined, and the frogs and other life were disturbed by a hurricane and flood. Research: Make a chart of temperatures and water events that affected animals and the food-making ability of green plants in New York and San Salvador.

INQUIRY CIRCLES

Inquiry circles, similar to literature circles, invite students to work together as they share the experience of reading and discussing nonfiction selections. As you set up inquiry circles, encourage topic selection and team building to make sure students stay motivated and engaged to successfully complete the task. Try a sequence of three guiding questions to help students discuss their readings with increasing complexity (see Figure 3.3). The three types of questions are definition questions, consequence questions, and action questions. These questions represent both multiple entry points into a discussion and varied levels of sophistication—cognitive and linguistic alike—required by the responder.

Keep in mind how important it is to engage students in a range of activities, projects, and authentic discussions that are student-directed as opposed to teacher-directed. Research consistently shows that when students have ownership of their

Guiding Questions for Inquiry Circles		FIGURE 3.3
Question Type	**Guiding Questions**	**Examples from readings about endangered species**
Definition Questions	What is it? What is taking place?	What is an endangered animal? What is happening to some animals around the world?
Consequence Questions	Why does it matter? Why is it important?	Why should we learn about endangered animals? Why does it matter if some species become extinct?
Action Questions	What can be done? What actions should be taken?	What actions can we take as individuals? What actions can our community take together?

learning, their academic performance and achievement improve (Hattie, 2012). One way to make the experience of the English learner more valuable is to offer enhanced opportunities for language acquisition in learning environments with high levels of challenge and rigor designed for partner work. Specifically, collaboration can help ELs practice and extend their oral discourse. It can also help them achieve a deeper understanding and more meaningful application of academic language. Similarly, ELs may have more chances to "try on" varied academic registers (Valdés, 2004).

Another partner arrangement is to develop collaborative assignments that are based on linguistically rich content discussions, such as social studies debates or scientific experiments. Frey and Fisher (2013) suggest that for groups to be most effective in learning, especially when reading and writing, they should comprise no more than six students. This gives teachers time to build partnerships with individual students as well as small groups. Students form inquiry groups based on self-selected topics of interest. The teachers act as mentors and guides who expertly facilitate the research process while also enthusiastically learn about the topic alongside their students. We have seen this in a 7th grade classroom where English learners selected unique, under-researched topics that allowed them to put their lives and experiences into the curriculum. Topics included cricket (the sport popular among Southeast Asian communities), securing fresh drinking water in sub-Saharan Africa, reducing air pollution in China, and saving coral in the Great Barrier Reef.

PROJECT-BASED LEARNING

Do you think about ways to engage your students, especially in content areas such as social studies and science? Project-based learning (Boss, 2015) is one way to support teams (teacher–student, student–student) and engage students by presenting a challenging question. Do you agree with Ashbrook (2019) when she states, "Having multiple experiences about a question, concept, or topic is more likely to happen if children become involved in an ongoing project" (p. 18)? We do! We also found that we must keep in mind all the key ingredients for successful teamwork (Larmer, 2015). Remember, you are the facilitator and the students are the problem solvers. That being the case

➤ Begin with a challenging problem or question that focuses students as they seek to find the answer(s).

➤ Develop sustained inquiry by using "thought starters" or student-generated questions so that students will continue to explore and work collaboratively to solve problems. The inquiry process happens over time, and deeper questions should be posed along the way.

➤ Ensure authenticity, as the problem and activities should reflect real life.

➤ Value student voice and choice to create ownership in the problem-solving process.

➤ Reflect on the shared experience so that students think about what they are learning.

➤ Keep in mind that critique and revision are elements of high-quality project-based learning and students should evaluate the results of their learning.

➤ Design a public product to display with the audience in mind.

One very effective way to meet the needs of your ELs is to implement project-based instruction while explicitly integrating content and language. Since there is a public display of the product at the end of the process, students are engaged in a community of learners (McDermott & Honigsfeld, 2017). There are extensive discussions, the sharing of ideas, formative assessments, and the development of deeper questions as students work toward their finished product. We find that ELs are highly motivated to share what they learned with their audience and often prefer a real-world, student-friendly, collaborative approach to learning. In one school we supported, teachers took the opportunity to co-develop essential questions for projects, brainstorm possible solutions, guide students (without over-powering them), and then design a culminating activity that was publicly displayed for parents and other members of the school to view in the building. Such rich interactions with complex materials and an authentic audience allow for consolidation of prior learning and an extension of new learning.

INQUIRY-BASED LEARNING AND PROJECT-BASED LEARNING: AN IMPORTANT DISTINCTION

Have you ever wondered what the similarities and differences are between inquiry-based learning and project-based learning?

In inquiry-based learning, students are generating questions and working with hands-on exploration. Generally, the student-centered exploration comes early in the lesson before any teacher-led instruction. This type of activity works very well for English learners because they are activating their prior knowledge.

In project-based learning, the focus is on the process as well as the end project or product. Students generally work in groups, and teachers have multiple opportunities to facilitate, model, and coach, all of which are especially helpful for English learners!

In both inquiry-based learning and project-based learning, the teacher–student partnership is crucial and must be grounded in trust so the ownership of learning can truly lie in the hands of the students.

IN CONVERSATION WITH TEACHERS

We asked teachers around the country the same questions: How do you build collaboration and partnerships between teachers and students? And, how do you successfully facilitate student learning while also nurturing independence? Here are three responses we received from exemplary elementary and secondary teachers.

Teachers Allyson Caudill (ESL), Ashley Blackley (1st grade), and John Cox (2nd grade) have a shared philosophy and common practice that they refer to as "microaffirmations":

Imagine you are 7 years old, back in elementary school, and the teacher just called on you to speak. You may have an answer in your head, but you are struggling to get it out with all eyes on you. Suddenly someone shouts, "You got this!" and the whole class joins in to cheer you on. Microaffirmations are one way that we have changed the culture in our classrooms and flipped the script. Students are consistently given feedback and encouraged by their peers, who call each other by name and use simple chants.

We greet students at the door every morning, and then they greet each other. These small acts motivate and reinforce a sense of community by making the accomplishments of an individual into success for the whole class. Included in this highly student-centered environment are built-in opportunities for student self-reflection and peer evaluation. Before we even evaluate the students, they evaluate themselves and each other with rubrics and utilize sentence frames to guide their constructive discourse.

Providing opportunities for students to practice academic language at the discourse level is a top priority for us. We provide the supports to get them there and then we allow them agency to carry on the conversations within the parameters. Often, students are the leaders in our classrooms. Students achieve more when they have the chance to lead, so we step aside and give them the floor whenever possible. Each day, a student leader launches the class with our morning song and reviews the classroom rules. Students beg to be chosen to administer the spelling test at the end of each week, love to lead the class in choral reading, guide the group in solving math equations, assist in developing the sentence frames used in academic discussions, and create and model action tricks for newly learned vocabulary. These are the main ways that we encourage students to collaborate and regularly use all four domains of language.

Brittany Schmidt and Carmen O'Brien, two 7th grade ELA teachers at Greenville Middle School in Greenville, Wisconsin, describe the unique way they introduced co-teaching in their school and how they helped enhance their middle school students' independence as learners:

We are fortunate to have a retractable wall between our two classrooms. This year, we have had it open most of the time and utilize this opportunity to combine our two classes and co-teach together. Our favorite co-teaching model in our combined class is station teaching, where we can carry out two teacher-led stations, two "focus skill" stations, and two independent reading/writing stations, depending on our unit. Students have praised this structure because it allows for movement, breaks, and targeted instruction during our ELA blocks. This structure has also transformed our instructional planning and delivery strategies. While all students benefit from this model, our EL students especially have excelled.

We can be purposeful in how we group students and are conscious that not all the EL students are in the same group all the time. When our EL students make it to the teacher-led stations, their speaking skills are put to the test in a small-group, nonthreatening environment. The teacher with that group can then give those ELs the individualized attention they need until they are confident enough to be independent in the next station. Since we teach our lessons together, we have become extremely familiar with our different teaching styles, and they have now evolved into their own unique forms. We are always aware of each other, and we are both seen as all 7th graders' ELA teachers.

LeKiesha White, biology teacher at Meadowbrook High School in Chesterfield County Public Schools, Virginia, describes her experience working with her sheltered ESL courses in respect to project-based learning:

When working with English learners, I have found that the students are ever curious about the real-world aspects of biology, as well as the concepts associated with the course. Through carefully planned project-based lessons with an inquiry component, ELs can expand their content knowledge pertaining to their everyday encounters. In our genetics unit, not only do they learn the foundational concepts of using Punnett Squares, but they can study their own familial physical traits to determine if they are recessive or dominant. In larger biology classes, challenges can arise, particularly with respect to content vocabulary. I have discovered, however, that project-based activities allow me to engage students from the start, using their "driving question." In these instances, the driving question allows me to pose a question to students to facilitate open dialogue, discuss vocabulary, activate prior knowledge, and establish a destination in our educational journey surrounding a specific topic.

Furthermore, I combine the practice of generating a driving question with the daily incorporation of vocabulary into our lessons. This is a practice that I encourage all educators to use when working with English learners. I call this framework the Frayer Model with a "twist." As a class, we develop a vocabulary book where each vocabulary word is written in both English and Spanish. This book also includes illustrations and definitions. Having strong content vocabulary is a premium and allows ELs to feel comfortable and confident in their learning. I have also discovered that students who have strong vocabulary exhibit success in the project-based learning model.

ELEMENTS FROM THE PROJECT-BASED LESSON MODEL TO ENSURE THE INQUIRY-BASED DIMENSION

These are some elements from the project-based lesson model to incorporate in your lesson template to ensure the inquiry-based dimensions and to strengthen the teacher–student partnership:

➤ A student-generated name for the project
➤ A clear description of the project and the duration that it may take to complete the project
➤ The driving question
➤ A list of resources needed to conduct inquiry
➤ A list of other subject areas that will be included to make the project interdisciplinary
➤ A summary of the project focusing on what the students have learned from hands-on research and inquiry
➤ A description of individual student contributions as well as group contributions
➤ A checklist as a reminder to the students of the four Cs of 21st century learning—collaboration, communication, creativity, and critical thinking

➤ A final product (as an assessment) that will be presented to the public and the teacher(s) to ensure that the learning objectives were met and the four Cs of 21st century learning were used

➤ An opportunity for reflection by the project team

➤ A list of future questions the students may still wish to research through problem solving

🕐 QUICK TIP 3: SURVEY YOUR STUDENTS!

Use student surveys to find out more about teacher–student partnerships. You can ask your students how they like to learn best: in large groups, in small groups, in teams, in pairs, alone, or one-on-one with a teacher or adult. Using the surveys and learning preferences as a springboard, you can decide which students welcome a strong teacher–student partnership and then model the helpful relationship. All students will learn from observing your positive partnership in a socially interactive, engaging environment and will benefit as well.

🧰 TECH TOOLBOX

Make use of technology tools and online resources that support collaboration between teachers and their students.

FLIPGRID

Do your students like to watch movies, make their own videos, or share videos with their friends and peers? If so, Flipgrid is a popular instructional strategy that enables students to record their own short videos on a topic they are learning about and then watch and reply to each other. This is one engaging way for your ELs to interact virtually and use more academic language.

NEARPOD

Through an interactive learning platform, this product offers lesson plans and supportive materials to create robust lessons in all subject areas, including digital citizenship and virtual reality.

POLLEVERYWHERE.COM

This teacher- and student-friendly website allows the teacher to gather real-time answers to questions. Through the Internet (Chromebooks, iPads, laptops, or phones [depending on age and resources]), students can respond to multiple-choice questions for a formative assessment or build a bar graph for their ideas.

CONCLUSION

As you read this chapter, did you think about the many ways that you forge a team approach to learning with your students? *Teaming up allows educators to cross the invisible boundaries between students and teachers.* Have you noticed that building partnerships leads to trusting relationships, which in turn enhance student engagement and collaboration inside and outside the classroom? Interactive learning, sparked with authentic questions and objectives fostered by teachers' genuine curiosity and interest in their students' lives, transforms the teaching-learning experience for all.

It is also striking that as students *team up* with their teachers, they find their voices and begin to *speak up*! Sharing ideas, solving problems, and offering diverse perspectives will lead English learners to *fire up* their class participation and take ownership of their learning.

Our hope is that when teachers and students are on the same team, there will be endless opportunities for academic success. Being on the same team means that varied educational collaborations and learning connections can be developed. Teaming can be the driving force that sparks innovative learning and engaging educational activities. Strong teams use language to communicate and share ideas, which maximizes the learning experiences of English learners.

Taking It Further: Reflection Questions

1. Do your teaming practices integrate ELs in your class? If so, how can you build on them? If not, how can you establish teaming as a priority?
2. Are you checking in with (taking the temperature of) your students often enough so you know how your teaching strategies are working? How connected do you feel to your students?
3. Have you tried inquiry-based learning or project-based learning? If so, which works best for your instruction? Which do you prefer and why? Where do you see the best student outcomes?

Additional Resources

Are you familiar with Colorín Colorado? This is one of the best available resources that serves teachers from preK to grade 12. This website is a guide for teachers and a resource of practical ideas for schoolwide support for English learners. Visit http://www.colorincolorado.org.

Do you access Teaching Channel to see simple and already proven teaching strategies? To see an amazing Teaching Channel video for teachers about science exploration through exploration and the 5E model, visit https://www.teachingchannel.org/videos/first-grade-science.

Do you want to find out more about project-based learning? Explore the Buck Institute website dedicated to this approach. Visit https://www.pblworks.org.

CHAPTER 4

TEACHER TEAMS AT THEIR BEST

Sustained teacher interaction is one of the most important factors in addressing the needs of students such as English learners.

Meredith Warren and Imani Davis were newly certified teachers who had been hired to join the math department of a small urban charter high school on the East Coast. The school's 354 students, 22 percent of whom were English learners, comprised mostly students of color. Colleagues in their department consisted of Frank Maranello, employed by the school the previous academic year, and Evelyn Rojas, a part-time staff support teacher who had been with the school for two years, taking on various roles—co-teacher, substitute teacher, individual or small-group instructor, and so on—as needed.

Both Meredith and Imani were impressed at their first faculty meeting by how the agenda was focused on shared responsibility to incorporate instructional strategies for the sake of English learners. The discussions that ensued during the course of the meeting invited everyone's ideas and perspectives, and the new teachers quickly appreciated how the whole school seemed to be part of an authentic collaborative community. In addition to the general faculty meetings held once per week, Meredith and Imani also participated in 45 minutes of collaboration time each morning with their department teams before students arrived.

The first week of their team meetings appeared to go very smoothly. Both Meredith and Imani got to know each other better, as well as the other two members of their department—Frank and Evelyn. Thereafter, they all spent a great deal of their collaboration time discussing some exciting and relevant topics, such as social-emotional learning, school choice, flipped classrooms, and student mental health, with some time allotted to talk about routine issues including class schedules, student discipline, grading papers, and so on. They quickly bonded over these conversations and offered support to one another. At the end of the first marking quarter, their assistant principal met with the team and asked them how they thought their collaboration had worked thus far to improve student learning. The new teachers shared how they appreciated the positivity and encouragement they felt from their colleagues and that they were at a loss as to how to relate their team meetings directly to student academic achievement.

Sustained teacher interaction is one of the most important factors in addressing the needs of students such as English learners, and having the time to collaborate during the school day increases the likelihood that new ideas will be shared and professional learning will occur. Yet, when new teachers such as Imani and Meredith, or seasoned teachers such as Frank and Evelyn, are unaccustomed to working in teams, the success of their collaborative efforts critically depends on establishing a common purpose and focusing on student growth and achievement. Purposeful interaction is essential; therefore, teachers need the training and support to focus on goal-setting activities that include examining student data, planning lessons together, reviewing assessment practices, sharing instructional resources, engaging in meaningful reflection, and so on to make the most of collaborative time.

In the previous chapters, we suggested creating collaborative classroom cultures in which students frequently work in small or large teams and where teachers take on the role of the facilitator supporting more student-directed work. We advocated for English learners to receive multiple meaningful opportunities to interact with each other, with their English-speaking peers, and with teachers for authentic academic language and literacy development.

In this chapter, we revisit the four core principles of teamwork and demonstrate how common purpose, shared mindset, supportive environment, and diverse team membership are critical components of teacher collaboration. As you read through this chapter, you will discover ways in which educators form cohesive teams to work more systemically in support of English learners' growth by answering the following key questions:

➤ *Who are your English learners?* Identify culturally and linguistically diverse student populations in your school and community.

➤ *What do you teach?* Examine the curriculum for culturally and linguistically responsive and sustaining content.

➤ *How do you teach?* Consider multimodal, multilingual, and multidimensional instructional strategies.

➤ *How do you assess?* Implement appropriate progress monitoring and formative and summative assessments.

➤ *How do you engage in thoughtful reflection on your teaching?* Choose a critical friend to partake in honest—sometimes difficult—conversations.

While these questions may serve as opportunities for individual teachers to grow, here we propose that combining teacher expertise and experiences, as well as looking through multiple perspectives, will multiply the impact you can have on all your students. We have lived by these principles for much of our professional lives and have collaborated with each other for more than a decade.

WHY TEACHER COLLABORATION?

Do you still remember when you were an aspiring teacher or perhaps when you were a student teacher? Do you still recall that formative experience when you first stood in front of a group of youngsters, ready to teach? Did it feel exhilarating, or lonely and scary, or a little bit of it all? Well, even if you felt that you were all alone in front of your first class, your teacher education professors were rooting for you in absentia, and your cooperating teacher was somewhere close by offering encouraging looks and nods. Teaching as a vocation is all about helping children grow and reach their full potential, so why wouldn't we also turn our profession into a more collaborative endeavor to help each other grow and reach our full potential in support of ELs? Effective collaboration among educators focuses on student growth and achievement as its main objectives. It encompasses targeted discussions, analysis of data, standards reviews, the co-construction of essential curricula, lesson planning, the development of assessment tools and techniques, and the thoughtful examination and re-examination of instructional delivery. It is sustained via the support of highly committed teachers and empowering school administrators (Honigsfeld & Dove, 2019).

In recent years, a substantial shift has occurred in English as a second language (ESL) or English language development (ELD) instructional and assessment practices. Developing academic language, general content-area literacy skills, and disciplinary literacy skills are recognized as critical for ELs to successfully participate in academic tasks (Gottlieb & Ernst-Slavit, 2014; Zacarian, 2013; Zwiers, 2014). It is increasingly commonly accepted that all teachers share the responsibility for engaging students in academic language practices and for building oral and written language skills closely tied to rigorous English language arts and content standards. As Gottlieb and Ernst-Slavit (2014) noted, teaching academic discourse is particularly important for "those students for whom English is a second, third, or fourth language and for students from underrepresented backgrounds who may not be surrounded by the types of thought and academic registers valued in schools" (p. 25). Therefore, it is essential for teachers to understand that cultural practices can impact students' readiness to learn, as well as how they are accustomed to learning. For this reason, researchers at WIDA (2014) also recognized, "Given the diversity of students and teachers, no isolated theory or approach is adequate to guide the learning and teaching of all language learners" (p. 6). Purposeful teacher collaboration for the sake of ELs holds a special promise for many reasons, including the following:

➤ Curriculum continuity with clear goals and objectives
➤ Instructional consistency that supports content and language development
➤ Reduction in fragmented, disjointed learning experiences for students
➤ Less student isolation and more integration into the school community

Purposeful teacher collaboration begins with developing an understanding of the expectations for teamwork, the adherence to the use of data-informed instruction, fidelity to congruent and inclusive learning experiences for all students, and the commitment to work in a coordinated manner. This way, teacher collaboration—embracing our collective knowledge and wisdom—can have a genuine basis for ongoing success.

CONSIDER THIS

There is an urgency to ensure that all teachers are prepared to work with ELs:

➤ English learners continue to be among the fastest-growing subgroups of preK–12 students, yet only a relatively small percentage of teachers are certified or trained in second language acquisition and multilingual and multiliteracy development.

➤ Even if schools have ELD classes or ELD specialists, ELs spend most of their day in the general education classrooms, so all teachers must be prepared to successfully teach ELs.

➤ Collaboration requires trust, so teachers must feel comfortable sharing what they know and what they do not know and must be willing to engage in critical reflections and joint professional learning.

Most of us will probably remember having one teacher in the room as the norm. Although it has been noted that "the long-standing culture of teacher isolation and individualism, together with teachers' preference to preserve their individual autonomy, may hinder deep-level collaboration" (Vangrieken, Dochy, Raes, & Kyndt, 2015, p. 36), research on teacher collaboration and its positive impacts have been emerging in the past couple of decades.

RESEARCH TO WATCH

➤ DuFour (2005) underscored the importance of collegial conversations because they enhance transparency among educators: Collaborative conversations call on team members to make public what has traditionally been private— goals, strategies, materials, pacing, questions, concerns, and results. These discussions give every teacher someone to turn to and talk to, and they are explicitly structured to improve the classroom practice of teachers—individually and collectively (p. 38).

➤ Kieffer, Lesaux, Rivera, and Francis (2009) conducted a comprehensive literature review in which they concluded, "Virtually all sophisticated academic tasks, such as solving complex mathematical problems or reasoning with scientific information, are mediated by language and literacy skills" (p. 1188). Since academic content learning and academic language development significantly overlap, we must treat the two in an integrated fashion and must imply that teacher collaboration allows for a deeper understanding of how language and content interplay with each other in rigorous academic contexts.

➤ Collaboration among teachers has been found to impact teaching quality, teacher retention, and job satisfaction among educators. Since we need highly qualified teachers who hold onto their jobs—and happily do so—the research of Burns and Darling Hammond (2014) reminds us of how critical teacher collaboration is. They found that "more than any other policy area, actions that support collaborative learning among teachers appear to hold promise for improving the quality of teaching" (p. v). If collaboration leads to higher level teaching, who will be ultimately served?

➤ More recently, DeLuca, Bolden, and Chan (2017) studied collaborative inquiry (CI) among teachers and concluded that it works best when certain relational or experiential factors were present, including "(a) teacher choice of inquiry focus; (b) acknowledging CI learning takes time; (c) acknowledging teachers as experts; (d) establishing trusting relationships with colleagues; and (e) seeing student success from CI" (p. 72). When teachers examine their teaching practices and their impact on student learning in collaboration, they learn together. And again, who will ultimately benefit? It is not just the participating teachers but their students as well who gain from teacher collaboration.

SOME KEY TERMS

The concepts we use in our discussions about teacher collaboration may be more or less familiar to you, depending upon the level of collaboration present in your schools. Across all classrooms, some might be new or used differently here. For the sake of clarity, here are definitions for the most common terms you may come across in the literature about collaboration for the sake of English learners:

➤ *Collaborative assessment.* Co-developing assessment tools and measures and collaboratively analyzing the data gleaned from those assessments.

➤ *Collaborative instructional cycle.* A continuous cycle of co-planning, co-teaching (if feasible), co-assessment, and reflection.

➤ *Collaborative inquiry.* A joint exploration of a shared problem of practice.

➤ *Co-teaching.* Two teachers co-delivering instruction in the same classroom.

➤ *Co-planning.* Two or more teachers taking joint responsibility for planning instruction for students that they may or may not co-teach.

➤ *Integrated content and language instruction.* An approach to teaching core-content classes that intentionally aligns subject matter goals with language and literacy development goals.

Moving from having a single teacher in a classroom who plans instruction and assessment alone to a comprehensive collaborative approach to serving all students' needs is a huge paradigm shift. Many schools have been on this path for years through the professional learning community (PLC) movement (DuFour & DuFour, 2012; Marzano, Warrick, Rains, & DuFour, 2018). Using the PLC movement as a point of reference, what we advocate for is a systemic approach to teacher collaboration for the sake of ELs—with a focus on student outcomes, a continuous examination of the data used to determine student learning, and a commitment to joint decision making as to how to respond to students' learning challenges. In other words, we strongly support creating and sustaining a school culture in which teacher collaboration is the norm and where all students can thrive.

UNPACKING THE COMMON FRAMEWORK

Continuing the format of the previous chapters, let's examine the overarching framework for this book from the vantage point of teacher collaboration:

➤ *Common Purpose.* When teachers come together to define success for all students, they build and sustain a community of practice around students' academic language and literacy development. You might perhaps

  ➢ Engage in continuous learning about culturally and linguistically diverse students and research-informed instruction.

➤ Make professional conversations about academic language and literacy development the norm.

➤ Become intentional about infusing language and literacy instruction into every lesson (not just during specially designated periods).

➤ Remain focused on providing an integrated and inclusive approach to learning for all students.

➤ *Shared Mindset.* When teachers commit to working together, they embrace an asset-based philosophy and a shared consciousness around the needs of their students and agree to

➤ Use an asset-based, shared language about ELs that captures what they can do rather than what they cannot do.

➤ Promote and support each other's collective learning about English learners.

➤ Break out of individual silos and share with each other what works, what has been tried, and what does not seem to work.

➤ Become advocates and stand up for ELs so they are provided with the instruction, resources, and services they need.

➤ Collectively problem solve the challenges each other faces teaching ELs by valuing diverse perspectives.

➤ *Diverse Team Membership.* When educators recognize the many different talents, the varied cultural and experiential backgrounds, and the rich practical experiences among themselves, they begin to

➤ See diversity as an asset and tap into colleagues' expertise.

➤ Engage in professional dialogue to seek and offer support to each other.

- ➤ Participate in formal and informal collaborative activities across grade levels, schools, and even districts.
- ➤ Form teams that consist of EL/ELD teachers and grade-level teachers (at the elementary level) or content-area teachers (at the secondary level).
- ➤ Establish sustainable structures and routines to ensure that collaborative teams become high-functioning units.

➤ *Supportive Environment.* When a culturally and linguistically welcoming school and classroom environment is developed, educators collectively plan ways to create a more inviting atmosphere for diverse students and their families. How can you accomplish this? You can perhaps

- ➤ Individually set professional learning goals for yourself to increase your knowledge and skills in order to work with diverse learners.
- ➤ Give up operating behind closed doors and welcome colleagues into your classes.
- ➤ Invite colleagues to be critical friends to discuss effective teaching for ELs.
- ➤ Share, share, share—success stories, how challenges were overcome, and what issues need to be addressed.

In case you are shaking your head slightly and thinking that this is all very nice and wondering how teachers can do it all without leadership support, we're there with you! Is collaboration the norm in your school? Do all (or at least most) teachers embrace it? Is it logistically well supported through time and resources? Leadership is critical to the success of any collaborative effort. If teachers are made to feel they are in competition with one another, they are more likely to protect their knowledge and skills and less likely to share them. If collaborative teams are not given adequate and consistent time to meet, their efforts will be less effective. If teachers are not given the needed resources to follow through with their plans, then any innovative instruction designed to meet the challenges of teaching ELs might not be accomplished. Having supportive school leaders that partner with their faculty is integral to establishing and sustaining vibrant teacher teams and effective teacher collaboration.

🕐 QUICK TIP 1: ESTABLISH A COLLABORATIVE APPROACH TO SERVING ELs

As a school community, establish clear expectations and set short-term and long-term goals for what a collaborative approach to serving ELs is supposed to look like. There is no one right way to achieve a cohesive, integrated service delivery model. We suggest you work in collaboration with each other to define the ways in which curricular continuity and instructional consistency may be achieved. Teacher ownership is key.

SEE IT IN ACTION

Teachers are notoriously short on time. In most schools we have visited and for most teachers we have interviewed, the number-one complaint is the lack of—or limited—available time for collaboration. We advocate for beginning with a master schedule that allows for ample weekly collaborative planning time with grade-level or subject-matter teams as well as with instructional specialists (such as EL/ELD teachers and other special service providers). In addition, putting peer support or coaching support in place prior to the beginning of the year will ensure in-class visits, co-planning, co-assessment, and reflection regularly occur. Four main focus areas we strongly advocate for to ensure flourishing and impactful collaboration are: (1) creating a supportive, inclusive school and classroom culture that values each student as a full member of the community; (2) developing curricula that carefully consider ELs' academic, linguistic, and literacy development; (3) integrating core-content instruction and language development goals; and (4) creating a fair, equitable, and collaborative assessment system for ELs and collaboratively assessing students' content and language development in both formative and summative ways (Dove, Honigsfeld, & Cohan, 2014). See Figure 4.1 for the four Cs of impactful teacher collaboration for the sake of ELs.

The Four Cs of Impactful Teacher Collaboration for ELs   FIGURE 4.1

Culture

Curriculum

Content and Language Integration

Collaborative Assessment

BUILDING AN INCLUSIVE CULTURE

Whose job is it to understand and respond to English learners' needs? It has been well established among both researchers and practitioners that responding to ELs' needs may not be the sole responsibility of the EL/ELD teacher (Staehr Fenner, 2013b). Students, to develop a strong sense of belonging, need to experience a whole group of caring, compassionate educators working in concert. Not only should we work in collaboration, we also need to engage in a cycle of professional learning, application of new learning, and shared reflection on what works and what does not in order to achieve further improvement of our practice.

A collaborative, inclusive school culture ensures that all teachers embrace a culturally responsive and sustaining philosophy, which is also more likely to break down cultural barriers and enhance cross-cultural communication among faculty, students, and families. Ladson-Billings (1995) was the first to propose a culturally relevant pedagogy, "a theoretical model that not only addresses student achievement but also helps students to accept and affirm their cultural identity while developing critical perspectives that challenge inequities that schools (and other institutions) perpetuate" (p. 469). Close to two decades later, Paris (2012) cautioned that cultural relevance may not be enough; instead, we must strive to create an environment in which each student is valued through a culturally sustaining pedagogy: "to maintain heritage ways and to value cultural and linguistic sharing across differences, to sustain and support bi- and multilingualism and bi- and multiculturalism" (p. 95).

A collaborative, inclusive environment is designed to fully integrate ELs with their English-speaking peers as well as students with a range of different abilities, thus also contributing to building a strong sense of community inside and outside of school. The alternative is no longer an option. Keeping ELs segregated by frequently removing them from the classroom for services or separating them in the classroom for lower-level work will only perpetuate stereotypes and myths about certain subgroups of students and about their likelihood to succeed academically. In order to fully integrate ELs, we suggest the following key strategies for building a collaborative, inclusive school culture:

➤ Engage in critical self-reflection individually and collectively around issues of equity and inclusion and challenge taken-for-granted assumptions.

   ➣ How to do it: Look around, walk around, listen around, and talk around issues of equity for English learners.

   ➣ Look Fors: Check to see if your ELs are fully included in their classrooms and the school community. Some questions to get you started: Can they see themselves in the curriculum? Are their home languages honored and considered an asset and a tool for learning? Are key resources and documents available in all the home languages represented in the school? Are ELs represented in school activities such as plays, clubs, student councils, and student government?

➤ Take a critical learning stance as educators.

   ➣ How to do it: Examine your own cultural and linguistic identity and family history as it compares with your students' and their families' lives. Share your stories with each other and your students.

   ➣ Look Fors: Listen for engaged conversations around identity and culture in the faculty room and at faculty meetings.

➤ Engage in collaborative inquiry around building an inclusive, collaborative school culture.

➤ How to do it: Initiate a more formal study and reflection through an equity audit (e.g., the one published by Staehr Fenner (2013a) focusing on key considerations, questions to ask, and implications for ELs).

➤ Look Fors: Some key elements include (1) appropriate placements based on proficiency levels; (2) ample opportunities for developing grade- and age-appropriate academic language and literacy skills; and (3) teaching and nonteaching school personnel such as guidance counselors, social workers, speech therapists, and psychologists working together to prioritize and respond to the needs of ELs.

➤ Find evidence of what works best for English learners.

➤ How to do it: Conduct participatory action research projects or collaborative lesson studies with your colleagues, or form teacher learning hubs and initiate an article study or book study on a topic of shared interest related to ELs.

➤ Look Fors: Examples of honest conversations about student growth, close examination of student data, careful analysis of student work samples, and shared teacher-made resources to provide differentiated instruction.

⏱ QUICK TIP 2: DEVELOP OWNERSHIP OF PROFESSIONAL LEARNING

Advocate for opportunities to co-construct the type of professional development that will best support teacher ownership of professional learning for effective instruction for ELs. Pay special attention to creating and sustaining learning partnerships to support

ELs' academic, linguistic, and social-emotional development. In one school, we supported teachers as they developed a year-long professional learning team that selected a series of practice-oriented articles, engaged in critical discussions around them, tried out key strategies, and monthly reported back to the team about how what they read and discussed informed their daily instruction—and what worked and what did not!

CURRICULUM WRITING, MAPPING, AND ALIGNMENT

The challenges are clear—if language development programs for English learners do not have a strong, purposeful connection to the grade-level content through curriculum alignment, what chance do ELs have to achieve high standards? On the flip side, if the core curriculum is not attentive to language and literacy development needs across content areas, what are the chances of systematic instruction and skills development? However, when you and your colleagues collaborate to review what is being taught and align the curriculum, the results are reflected in the shared academic and literacy goals and the identification of instructional strategies, materials, and differentiated learning tasks by all teachers.

English learners typically need to make more than a year's progress to graduate on time and be on par with their English-speaking peers. What we teach and how we plan instruction will have a major impact on how steadily ELs progress. A carefully crafted, *accelerated* curriculum is a powerful tool to achieve the necessary knowledge and skills ELs need to make adequate progress. Most curriculum maps include five types of essential information: the content; the standard that is addressed in the curricular unit; the processes and skills needed to learn the content; the key formative and summative assessment tools; and the main resources used in the unit. These five components seem pretty straightforward, correct? Yet, what is glaringly absent from such a map is understanding the unique needs of ELs. So, what we strongly advocate for is including language and literacy goals aligned to the core content and strategic accommodations and modifications for ELs in light of their language proficiency levels.

Curriculum writing, mapping, and alignment are fundamental parts of any school's approach in support of ELs regardless of the English language development program model in effect. Engaging in collaborative curriculum planning and alignment work also ensures a more cohesive, collaborative instructional cycle that consists of co-planning, co-teaching, co-assessment, and reflection. Schmoker (2009), as a long-time advocate for the Professional Learning Communities movement, reminds us, "Authentic teams build effective curriculum-based lessons and units together—which they routinely refine together on the basis of common assessment data" (p. 527). Teams also need to be intentional about honoring students' diverse cultural, linguistic, and literacy experiences when writing curriculum. Key strategies and tools for curriculum mapping and alignment include

➤ Recording and reviewing what the intended curriculum is and what is actually being taught.

➤ Ensuring that your students see themselves, their literacy experiences, and their personal lives in the academic content.

➤ Designing core-content curricula (math, science, English language arts, and social studies) as well as specialized curricula (music, arts, and technical subjects) that include students' cultures.

➤ Adding multimodal and multilingual resources to ensure that ELs can successfully meet grade-level, core-curricular goals.

INTEGRATED CONTENT AND LANGUAGE INSTRUCTION

When you teach math, you also teach the complex language of integers, coefficients, equations—or simply, the language of mathematics. When you conduct a science experiment and you have your students carefully read the steps of the process followed by a lab report, you expect them to read and write as scientists. The language and literacy skills needed for social studies vastly differ from those in the other subjects, including the visual arts, music, home and career studies, technology, and so on. While many English learners acquire conversational, everyday communication skills with relative ease, developing their academic language is no small feat! You might have heard that it takes much longer to become proficient in academic English due to the complexity of language used in each subject matter and the comprehensive literacy skills needed to do well in each content area.

When Cummins and Early (2015) systematically identified the linguistic demands of math, science, social studies, and English language arts, they argued that the rich and highly specialized vocabulary, the syntactic complexity of long sentences, and the density of texts across a variety of topics and genres present unique challenges to even more proficient ELs. However, they also emphatically claimed that "there is also no justification for excluding students from academic content learning for the more than five years it may take them to fully acquire academic English" (p. 85). The choice is clear: content and language must be taught simultaneously while using highly effective strategies to ensure students have access to grade-level content.

Integrated content and language instruction also suggests that all teachers have a mutual understanding of the content-based and language-development goals ELs must meet. When you look at your curriculum map, spacing guide, or an upcoming unit or lesson plan, do you consider both the academic (or cognitive) demands and the linguistic (or literacy) demands of the core content your students need to master? Looking through those two lenses allows for an integrated approach to teaching any subject.

Consider the following key strategies for content and language integration:

➤ Establish consistently high standards and high expectations for your ELs regarding content attainment, regardless of language proficiency levels.

➤ Make a conscious effort to include your English learners' rich and diverse lived experiences in your lessons through stories, images, student research opportunities, and connections to historical and current events.

➤ Have students make frequent authentic, real-life connections between what they already know and what they are learning in school.

➤ Be strategic about the vocabulary and sentence structures that are emphasized to promote language and literacy development. That is, make sure ELs understand what is being taught while simultaneously challenging them to take risks and expand their comfort zones.

➤ Develop and assess content- and language-development goals and objectives and plan units and lessons that are responsive to the data you are collecting on your ELs.

🕐 QUICK TIP 3: EMBRACE *MULTIPLE* WAYS TO INTEGRATE CONTENT AND LANGUAGE

Think of the prefix "multi" as a way to remember meaningful ways to integrate content and language for ELs. Instruction should be multimodal, multilingual, and multisensory with with multiple entry points into the rigorous curriculum and with multiple types of supports to manage the complex skills of the content.

Make sure ELs use technology to access information through videos (with subtitles in English or their native languages), images, and multilevel texts (e.g., try www.newsela.com). Accelerate ELs' learning by helping them express themselves through different modalities and tools before they are fluent in English.

FAIR AND EQUITABLE COLLABORATIVE ASSESSMENT PRACTICES

When you look at work produced by your English learners, what captures your attention at first glance? We embrace an asset-based approach that focuses on what the students can do, what we as their teachers can build on, and what supports are needed to help them reach the next level of standards. We believe that assessment of ELs must consider their individual strengths as well as academic and linguistic development that captures their growth rather than deficiencies. A fair and equitable assessment system for ELs will include a collaborative approach to assessment *as, for*, and *of* learning (Gottlieb & Honigsfeld, 2019):

➤ Assessment *as* learning offers your students opportunities to reflect on and assess their own academic and linguistic performance and progress, as well as to set content and language learning goals.

➤ Assessment *for* learning is formative and ongoing in nature, and it helps establish instructional goals and objectives for your units and lessons. This practice also aids in deciding whether there is a need to further build your students' background knowledge or the requisite for reteaching and review.

➤ Assessment *of* learning refers to summative assessment practices that help establish whether students have met unit goals, benchmarks, or end-of-year expectations, as well as how well they may be doing on standardized assessments.

To gather the most accurate, comprehensive, and meaningful data about your students' academic and linguistic development, make sure assessment *as*, *for*, and *of* learning are all part of your practice. When you coordinate the use of multiple data sources and multiple modes of assessments, the data will reveal how well your students are doing. For example, a range of formal and informal assessments including all four language skills—listening, speaking, reading, and writing across the content areas—may best determine individual students' needs and be used more effectively for planning follow-up and continued instruction.

Collaborative assessment for ELs' linguistic, academic, and literacy development may range from working in collaboration to prepare assessment tasks (what the students will be doing), assessment tools (what checklists, rubrics, ratings scales, or other tools you or the English-speaking students will be using), and assessment measures (what criteria will be used to determine success). When you collaborate with your colleagues around assessment practices, consider the following recommendations for student assessment (Honigsfeld & Dove, 2019):

➤ Vary assessment tasks and tools so that ELs are able to demonstrate their knowledge, abilities, and skills in addition to their language and literacy competencies.

➤ As an alternative to traditional assessments, establish individual assessment portfolios containing samples of ELs' work that illustrate their growth over a period of time.

➤ Support ELs' success by adapting assessments to include drawings, charts, word boxes, reduced amounts of text, simplified directions, multilingual support, and so on.

➤ Allow the use of print and online resources, such as bilingual dictionaries, thesauri, and class notes during test taking.

➤ Arrange for ELs to have extended time to complete assessments.

➤ Create opportunities in which ELs share what they know one-on-one or in small groups with their peers and teachers.

➤ Take anecdotal notes of individual ELs' progress and learning challenges and share them with your colleagues as appropriate.

➤ Devise assessment tools—rubrics, checklists, guidelines, peer reviews, and so on—to gather performance data and promote student self-assessment.

One ESOL teacher we worked with made a special effort to collaborate with all three grade-level teachers who had ELs in their classes. He developed a Google document that enabled him to collect anecdotal records, brief narratives, and more measurable data collections across the core content areas (via checklists, rubrics, and ratings scales). He was able to share his findings and work with his colleagues to monitor the students' progress. In addition, he had a weekly goal-setting template that also elicited student input.

 # QUICK TIP 4: PROVIDE ASSESSMENT ACCOMMODATIONS

Don't be afraid to use a range of accommodations on content assessments. For example, reduce the number of multiple-choice distractors and add visuals, a word box, or a bilingual glossary. You will be pleased to see that lower language proficiency levels may not impede your ELs from showing what they know about the target content when adequate supports are available.

IN CONVERSATION WITH TEACHERS

We asked educators around the country the same question: How do you collaborate with your colleagues to impact student learning with a special emphasis on supporting English learners? Here are three powerful responses we would like to showcase. As you read them, consider how they may be applicable in your own context.

Michelle Makus Shory, high school ESL resource teacher, and Irina McGrath, middle school ESL instructional coach in the Jefferson County Public Schools, Kentucky, share their collaborative coaching experiences:

> *Two years ago, our instructional office decided to team up and co-create and co-facilitate professional learning opportunities for teachers and bilingual instructors. Our decision stemmed from our beliefs in flexibility and choice. We knew that teachers had busy lives in and out of school. Therefore, we decided to offer two professional development (PD) formats that were grounded in key practices that support language and content development of English learners. Two of our colleagues committed to providing face-to-face sessions while we took on a new PD initiative to bring online and face-to-face technology for ELs to our district. We challenged ourselves to try new platforms and earn Google certifications. We scoured Twitter for fresh ideas and tools and read countless articles and books in order to find the very best resources for teachers. The true beauty of this experience was the joy of bringing our ideas together and co-creating in the most supportive and professional way. We believe this genuine spirit of collaboration was contagious. Our online community has*

become a safe place to share ideas, ask questions, and celebrate successes. We now have an active Twitter presence—#JCPSEL—that promotes and supports teachers and coaches, and we like to think that maybe our instructional team's collaborative approach played a small part in the growth of our district community. Working together and learning from each other has become one of the most professionally fulfilling experiences of our careers, and it has impacted our students in positive ways.

Erin Lee Holtkamp, ENL teacher in the West Hempstead Union Free School District, and Kristin Rochford, 1st grade teacher in Bethpage Union Free School District, share their unique story of collaboration across district lines through their shared connection to their alma mater:

Our story began with a yearning for collaboration, friendship, and love for teaching with technology! We began our journey after connecting during a Molloy College, Rockville Centre, NY, For Us By Us conference. We were working in different school districts on Long Island, teaching kindergarten and first grade. After reaching out to each other for guidance and support during our first few months in the classroom, we quickly realized we had much in common and that we shared very similar teaching philosophies.

Together we decided to incorporate different teaching strategies and technology tools in our classrooms to connect our classes as video pen pals. This also gave us the opportunity to collaborate as alumni and colleagues outside our classroom walls. We used Flipgrid as a teaching tool to engage and connect our students virtually; this was the driving force of our project. We also used Google

Drive to share resources and ideas and as a source of support. Our students were paired up, quickly introduced via Flipgrid, and were soon writing letters to each other. We even connected our schools' writers workshop curriculum to bring opinion-letter writing into the project. It was truly amazing to see how much these kinders and firsties could learn from each other in such a short time. We combined creative connections using technology, curriculum, and student voice.

Our project truly came to life when we connected at Molloy College for a STEM LEGO collaboration field trip. Not only did our students get to meet face to face, they got to experience the school their teachers had called home for so long and work with their video pen pals to code LEGO creatures they created. This was a "full circle" experience for us. It was wonderful to bring our students together and share a school experience that is so close to our hearts. With a little hard work, friendship, and collaboration, anything is possible! We have both become better friends and educators because of this experience. Our students also benefitted through multiple meaningful, authentic interactions.

Tanya L. Franca, former K–12 ESOL coordinator in Berkeley County School District, South Carolina, shared her story of including administrative leadership to support a new co-teaching initiative:

Knowing, understanding, and implementing best practices for ELs is never fully effective in a silo. All successful aspects of education are most effective and far-reaching when created and implemented by a collaborative team with the same vision and drive. Collaborative and high-functioning teams are not just for teachers; they are also for school and district leaders. As the K–12 ESOL coordinator for a district of 4,000 ELs, I cannot achieve much for the program, teachers, and students working alone. I began the journey three years ago by building relationships with school leaders across the district. All of us recognized the need for EL support, and soon I was able to organize a solution to fill that need and gap. We knew a change had to be made. Notice the word was "we." We collaboratively created a goal and then a plan to achieve it at our various schools. For our district, the solution became co-teaching with English learners. In five of our high-EL-populated elementary schools, this became a major service model shift. With a common goal, a strong commitment, and the right support, we are determined to make it happen. Most important, our vision is not for a short, one-year commitment but a true and full investment over time that will reap amazing results. Amid all the limitations, we collaboratively worked as leaders to make a real change that we know will positively affect EL success.

⏱ QUICK TIP 5: DECIDE COLLABORATIVELY THE MEANING OF CO-TEACHING FOR ELs

If you have the opportunity to engage in co-teaching, co-construct the meaning of what co-teaching for ELs should be. Make sure you develop a shared understanding of what it sounds and looks like in the classroom, and what collaborative practices are needed for it to be successful. (Hint: Co-planning, co-assessment, and reflection are often cited requisites).

TECH TOOLBOX

Offer training and secure technology platforms for all teachers to have access to curriculum guides, curriculum maps, and online co-planning tools.

GOOGLE DRIVE

Although Google is most known as a search engine that also offers cloud-based file storage, Google Drive also serves as an excellent tool for collaboration. You can share folders and files and collaborate on creating and editing shared documents. Using additional Google tools (such as sharing a classroom or engaging in conference calls via Google Hangouts) is also helpful.

DROPBOX

While Dropbox looks like and works like any other folder on your computer, it also allows you to sync all files to an online folder. Dropbox becomes a powerful collaboration tools when you share some of your subfolders with others. If any changes are made on one device, the files are automatically synced and are accessible on any other computer to which your account is linked.

MICROSOFT ONEDRIVE

OneDrive is similar to Google Drive in that it works as a cloud-based storage and file-sharing system as well as a collaboration tool. All other Microsoft products are also easily integrated into OneDrive.

CONCLUSION

When teachers team up, they are better able to engage in continuous learning about English learners by focusing their professional conversations on how to best incorporate language and literacy development into each lesson. In doing so, they can develop mutual knowledge about the needs of ELs, as well as develop better ways to meet instructional challenges by sharing what works and what doesn't. When teachers collaborate, they often feel empowered to speak up and become advocates for ELs so that they obtain the instruction, resources, and services they need. Collectively, teachers can also establish sustainable ways to be a meaningful force for change and create a welcoming school environment for diverse students and their families.

Taking It Further: Reflection Questions

1. From your own experiences, in what ways has leadership mattered when building diverse team membership?
2. What are some elements of a supportive environment that you and your colleagues will need to foster collaboration in your school or with the community?
3. Have you made it part of your regular practice to speak up in your school on behalf of your English language learners to meet their needs? If so, how?

Additional Resources

Have you ever explored co-teaching for ELs? A website created by Dr. Maria G. Dove and Dr. Andrea Honigsfeld provides detailed information about collaboration and best coteaching practices for English language learners. Visit www.coteachingforells.weebly.com.

Do you want to read authentic stories of teachers who build teams? For a website with multiple blog posts that focus on collaborative practices, visit www.readysetcoteach.com.

Do you serve a large number of diverse students, and are you concerned about taking steps to create an equitable learning environment for all? For equity-focused resources, visit https://www.icsequity.org.

CHAPTER 5

FIRED UP TO SUPPORT ELs: TEAMS THAT EXTEND BEYOND THE CLASSROOM

Leveraging community members and their
assets ... is one powerful way to connect
families, communities, and schools.

A child-study team meeting was being held to determine the educational needs of a 2nd grader who had been making inadequate progress with grade-level reading and language skills even though she had been communicative with her peers and participated in all academic conversations in the classroom. She had been attending the school since kindergarten, and her grade-level teacher, Ms. Carmen Deandrea, had become concerned because the child, Mehreen, was not making progress despite carefully designed, tiered interventions. Her parents, Amar and Bahra Khan, joined the meeting shortly before it began and were greeted by the principal, Ms. Sydney Moore, and the many team members—the psychologist, the special education teacher, the speech therapist, and the occupational therapist. The grade-level teacher was delayed because her substitute was late in arriving.

Mr. and Mrs. Khan were a bit overwhelmed by the number of people in the room; they sat quietly with concerned looks on their faces. Ms. Moore called for the meeting to begin and asked the team if it was necessary to call the phone translation service they use for Urdu-speaking parents. At that moment, the speech therapist recognized the Khans as the owners of the local coffee shop she frequented. She greeted the Khans warmly and began to chat with them about their children and the new bookstore opening next to their shop. The Khans started to relax when another familiar face, Ms. Deandrea, entered the room. She shook both of their hands, sat next to the Khans, and began to share something their daughter said in class that morning.

It quickly became obvious to the principal that not only did the Khans not need a translator, but they also could be a schoolwide, community asset when she learned that they were also proficient in several other languages in addition to English and Urdu. After a successful meeting, Ms. Moore approached the Khans with an idea. She explained that there were a number of families who had children in their school that spoke a language other than English. She wondered if they might at times consider acting as a liaison between parents and school, helping families to better understand the process involved in obtaining special education and other services.

When the Khan family arrived at the school, they were quite apprehensive about the child-study team meeting, and it appeared as if they felt like outsiders in a room full of strangers. However, when they were warmly greeted by the principal and the speech therapist and then by a teacher and were acknowledged for their multi-lingual skills, their apprehension faded and they began to feel welcomed. When Ms. Moore approached the Khans about helping other families, she was, in essence, asking them to become an integral part of the school community by serving as cultural brokers for the school. Leveraging community members such as the Khan family and their assets is one powerful way to connect families, communities, and schools.

Imagine that you are a young parent picking up your child for the first time from your neighborhood elementary school situated a few blocks away from your new home. As you approach the building, you notice that there is a vast amount of security in place—the area is completely gated off from the rest of the community and there is only one way in and one way out of the school campus. You climb the steps to enter the building and the doors are locked. A voice over an intercom alerts you to a glass booth on your left and an office assistant speaks to you through closed windows via a microphone. You begin to realize that parents are not allowed in the building, and you are pointed in the direction of the correct exit to wait for your child. Now imagine that you are an immigrant parent who speaks little or no English and whose access to teachers and their students in the past had always been readily welcomed. What would your first impressions of your child's new school be?

With the safety and security of children in mind, many schools seem to have become more remote from the greater community and more bureaucratic when dealing with rules, regulations, and restricted access. However, what schools need most, in addition to safe environments, is to create *welcoming* environments for families of all students to provide appropriate supports for children to thrive. There is an imperative for schools to make authentic connections with the communities they serve to foster relationships and nurture family partnerships for successful student outcomes, particularly with families who speak languages other than English.

In previous chapters, we have stayed within the boundaries of the classroom, school, and district contexts and explored what teaming and collaboration do to support ELs. We have highlighted positive practices and empowering strategies to fully engage all students in the personal, cultural, linguistic, and academic learning experiences.

In this chapter, we will expand our discussion of the four core principles of teamwork to the larger context of ELs' parents and neighborhood communities and show how common purpose, shared mindset, diverse team membership, and supportive environment serve as the pillars for community engagement. As you immerse yourself in this chapter, you will uncover successful practices for school, family, and community collaboration with a special emphasis on valuing the contributions of, and fully including, culturally and linguistically diverse students.

WHY COMMUNITY ENGAGEMENT?

Pause for a moment to recall what the neighborhood you grew up in was like. What are some of the most vivid memories you recall? Is it a bicycle ride after school every day with neighborhood friends? Is it staying late after school or going to the local library for chess club? Is it hanging out at the corner candy store? Did any of your memories have anything to do with members of your community looking out for you and other children, keeping tabs on who was doing what and where? While communities constantly change and sociocultural factors such as technology have been reshaping how our youths spend time after school, members of each community deeply care about their children and represent an often-untapped resource—parents and community members who may not be well connected to the local school or district.

A Sukuma proverb is well suited to offer inspiration to reaching and engaging the entire community in ELs' education: *One knee does not bring up a child.* When educators within a school community see families as a resource and a partner, they reach out and invest in building a bridge. When families see the school as a resource and a place to trust, they develop a bond and forge community relationships. Epstein and Associates (2019) refer to this as *family-like schools*—where teachers value each child for whom he or she is as parents and caregivers would—and *school-like families*—who support their children's education by working in tandem with the teachers. Take time to establish these relationships!

In family-like schools, teachers make each child feel special—just as parents do (e.g., asking on a Monday morning about the student's weekend soccer game or welcoming back to class in a special way a student who was home sick for a few days). Similarly, in school-like families, parents may ask how school was that day, what activity or subject the child likes best, or if they need any books or resources. The results from building these relationships are increased self-confidence for students, stronger connections to school life, more engaged families, and multiple sources of support for the English learner.

CONSIDER THIS

➤ If we accept that parents are their children's first and most important teachers, how can we seek input when designing culturally and linguistically responsive and sustaining curriculum and instruction for their children?

➤ Let's tap into the universal theme that parents have a desire to be role models for their children and want the very best for them. They can also offer insights and provide information regarding household routines that may impact studying or the ability to do homework. One way to strengthen the bonds between parents, students, and teachers is to encourage parents to share how they think their children learn best.

➤ English learners bring rich linguistic, literacy, and cultural experiences passed down from their immediate or extended family and community members. How can we embrace these cultural assets and what needs to be in place so that we all commit to valuing and building on them?

➤ Schools can better reflect the communities they serve with purposeful planning! How can we ensure that the community becomes a core source of information and support? How can we establish a pathway for external sources to enter the schools, both tangibly (resources, materials, and donations) and intangibly (parent, family, and community participation in the academic lives of children through field trips, assemblies, class visits, and community events)?

➤ Some families within any given school may feel disengaged and marginalized (Ferlazzo, 2011) when they do not fully understand what the school norms and expectations are. In what ways can teachers and administrators ensure that all families feel fully included and actively engaged in shaping the cultural fabric of the school?

Families and community members in collaboration with teachers and administrators need to establish a culture of caring, mutual respect, and productive collaboration. We, as do many others, carefully choose our words to describe community engagement rather than involvement: engagement requires full and equitable contributions, whereas involvement indicates a lack of shared decision making (Ferlazzo, 2011).

Traditionally, parents and primary caregivers are invited to school for open houses, back-to-school nights, parent–teacher conferences, sit-in-your-child's-seat events, Parent Teacher Association (PTA) meetings, and board meetings. While these are important activities in which to involve parents, they remain one-directional and are often initiated by the school. At the same time, Zacarian and Silverstone (2015) remind us, "Some families may feel that they are not welcome, have no voice, and/or are rejected by other families" (p. 27). When parents and families feel marginalized, their children will sense an uneasy feeling, may not believe they are in a safe and trusting environment, and may not value the spirit of school relationships. Therefore, it is crucial that teachers and school officials figure out ways to invite and sustain relationships with students and their families—including extended families! It's time to fire up the family spirit in support of learning.

RESEARCH TO WATCH

➤ Paris (2012) carefully reviewed and critiqued decades of research on culturally responsive (Ladson-Billings, 1995; 2014) or proficient pedagogy and argued that they fall short on making the much-needed difference in engaging EL families. Instead, he proposes culturally sustaining pedagogy defined as "supporting multilingualism and multiculturalism in practice and perspective for students and teachers. That is, culturally sustaining pedagogy seeks to perpetuate and foster—to sustain—linguistic, literate, and cultural pluralism as part of the democratic project of schooling" (Paris, 2012, p. 93). Paris and Alim (2017) went further and translated this research into a comprehensive set of practical applications for the K–12 school and classroom context.

➤ Ishimaru and her colleagues (2016) examined how "individuals who serve as *cultural brokers* play critical, though complex, roles bridging between schools and families" (p. 1). They also noted that formal leadership "enabled more collective, relational, or reciprocal cultural brokering. These dynamics suggest potential stepping-stones and organizational conditions for moving toward more equitable forms of family-school collaboration and systemic transformation" (p. 1).

➤ Takanishi and Le Menestrel (2017) reported national survey results about family engagement among EL parents and synthesized what practices are in place in school communities with higher levels of EL parent engagement:

> Creating a welcoming environment, providing orientation programs, using technology to enhance two-way communication, instituting district- and school-level parent advisory committees and school support teams that include parents of ELs to support ELs' academic success and emotional well-being, and instituting adult education programs for parents of ELs." (p. 281)

Additionally, schools can offer free or low-cost adult education classes for basic literacy, job readiness, and so on.

🔑 SOME KEY TERMS

School and family partnerships are among the most frequently discussed challenges when it comes to working with ELs and their families. As in all previous chapters, our goal here is to ensure a shared understanding of some essential terms.

➤ *Advocacy.* Action on behalf of those impacted by injustice or inequity.

➤ *Community.* A group of people who share a sense of belonging together.

➤ *Cultural brokers.* Individuals who help families understand and decode the unfamiliar school culture and create a bridge between cultural groups.

➤ *Family.* The nuclear family of parents and children has a revised definition that includes extended family members, guardians, siblings, or step-siblings and may even include close family friends.

➤ *Involvement versus engagement.* Involvement indicates a one-way street—schools involve parents but only when and if invited. Engagement offers opportunities for full and equitable participation of parents and families in schools.

➤ *Interculturalism.* Interaction between and among diverse groups of people with varied cultural backgrounds.

➤ *Multilingual.* Communicating in two or more languages or dialects.

➤ *Multimodal.* Using two or more modalities, such as text-based and visual- or image-based communication tools.

UNPACKING THE COMMON FRAMEWORK

Utilizing the common framework established for this book, let's see how collaborative engagement by parents and families may support ELs' academic, linguistic, and social-emotional learning:

➤ *Common Purpose.* When educators, parents, and community members come together to define success for all students, they work together with a commitment that is future-minded and goal-oriented. You might perhaps

  ➢ Articulate what life- and world-readiness are for preK–12 students.

  ➢ Consider students' and families' immediate and long-term needs.

  ➢ Ensure that the curriculum and in- and out-of-school learning experiences include authentic, real-world outcomes.

  ➢ Accelerate rather than remediate the academic learning for ELs.

➤ *Shared Mindset.* When educators, parents, and community members commit to working together, they

> ➤ Develop a shared ownership of education that highlights the school's positive learning environment and the availability of successful, quality education for English learners.
> ➤ Firmly believe that together they can do better for all students and their families.
> ➤ Create a shared vision and mission statement for the school and the school district (and possibly include community organizations or local coalitions).
> ➤ Share information and communicate openly, with the students' best interest in mind.
> ➤ Foster relevant and cross-cultural conversations that help build better understanding of one another's backgrounds and stories.
> ➤ Advocate on behalf of students without personal or political agendas.

➤ *Diverse Team Membership.* When educators, parents, and community members regularly and meaningfully collaborate with each other across racial, ethnic, linguistic, and other cultural lines, they

> ➤ Benefit from diverse experiences and shared cultural understandings.
> ➤ Model collaboration and civic participation for the children and youths of the school and community.
> ➤ Learn from others' expertise and knowledge.
> ➤ Grow as learners and teachers.
> ➤ Respond directly to community needs using positive and enthusiastic language.
> ➤ Help students find future educational opportunities and face educational challenges.

➤ *Supportive Environment.* When educators, parents, and community members contribute to creating a culturally and linguistically welcoming school and classroom environment, they establish a culture of inclusivity (which may take time and effort). How can you accomplish this?

> - Create multiple meaningful opportunities for inter-actions across cultural and linguistic boundaries.
> - Develop, with community input, instructional tech-niques that are culturally and linguistically respon-sive to community needs.
> - Select curriculum that reflects the students and their families and present it in an accurate and positive manner.
> - Secure resources that benefit a supportive learning environment.

Collaborative community and parent engagement may be established within the entire school district or more closely con-nected to an individual school. Both district and school building leaders play an essential role in being viewed and accepted as members of the larger community. In neighborhood schools where educators live in the same community as the children and families they serve, teachers and leaders are visible across all contexts—they shop in the same stores, attend the same places of worship, frequent the same businesses, and so on. In most communities, though, educators may not reside in the same zip code as the children and families they serve. However, this does not have to mean a disconnected relationship from the com-munity. There are many opportunities for you to support your community through after-school activities such as community-sponsored baseball or soccer leagues, attending a block party, attending local political events or walk-a-thons, or joining the Memorial Day parade. Visibility counts! We must see "the fuller, more complicated realities of these students' lives" (Gutiérrez & Orellana, 2006, p. 504), and to better understand their lived experiences, we had better advocate for them and help them advocate for themselves!

SEE IT IN ACTION

There are several key approaches to creating enhanced school, family, and community collaboration. Here we strongly advocate for five essential actions you can take: (1) create a safe and supportive learning environment, (2) make resources and communication multilingual and multimodal, (3) establish partnerships with community-based organizations, (4) encourage advocacy and parent leadership, and (5) tell your story to make success visible (See Figure 5.1).

Essential Actions to Create Enhanced School, Family, and Community Collaboration FIGURE 5.1

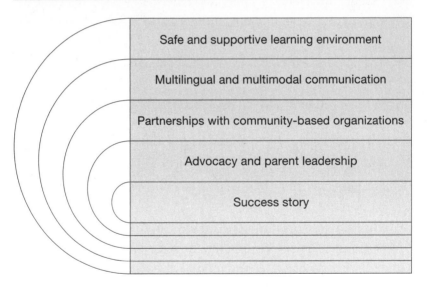

Safe and supportive learning environment

Multilingual and multimodal communication

Partnerships with community-based organizations

Advocacy and parent leadership

Success story

A SAFE AND SUPPORTIVE LEARNING ENVIRONMENT FOR ALL

What would you consider the most important part of sending your children off to school? Do you agree that first and foremost, children must feel safe and supported in school and families must feel safe coming to the school and supported in their efforts to raise their children? A heathy environment—one that supports all learners in their physical, academic, linguistic, and social-emotional development—must be a firm baseline. What does such an environment look like? Here are some of the best practices that we have observed:

➤ Students and families are treated with dignity, compassion, and respect.

➤ Parents and family members are welcomed to the school and greeted warmly.

➤ Parents know their children's teachers and administrators and where to reach them.

➤ Parents are familiar with classroom routines and room numbers.

➤ Parents are aware of safety and emergency procedures at the school and have contact numbers and e-mail addresses for those responsible for their children.

➤ Translators are available for school events, including parent–teacher conferences.

➤ Parents understand special programs or teaching configurations that benefit their child, such as co-teaching partnerships, response to intervention programs, and holiday events.

➤ Parents have input into school concerns through reliable lines of communication.

➤ Principals respect and encourage family feedback and try to respond to questions in a timely and meaningful manner.

Mapp (2003) explains that when "parents have caring and trusting relationships with school staff, these relationships enhance their desire to be involved and influence how they participate in their children's educational development" (p. 36). In short, for a family and school to have a successful partnership, there must be strong levels of commitment, meaningful communication, and trust. What is your vision of family engagement?

MULTILINGUAL AND MULTIMODAL RESOURCES AND COMMUNICATION

Is a language other than English within a community considered a barrier or a resource? Do diverse racial and ethnic groups feel welcomed in the school, and do they have opportunities for full participation? Let's take on the challenge of posing these key questions and strive to create an inviting and open learning environment. One way to ensure that everyone has access to information, resources, and participation is to centralize information through a school website or newsletter. If English is not the language spoken at home, then all the flyers stuffed into backpacks may pile up until they can be translated. Using a centralized system that has multilanguage translations available meets the immediate needs of families, and important items such as early dismissals can be highlighted. "A major concern is that some parents know how to speak the language of schooling and thus provide an advantage for their children during the school years, and others do not know this language, which can be a major barrier to the home making a contribution to achievement" (Hattie, 2009, p. 61). Helping parents navigate the educational system is a gift that benefits all students who are English learners. Speak the language that the parents speak. See Figure 5.2 for a parent welcome letter in two languages.

Welcome Letter in Two Languages

FIGURE 5.2

Freeport Public Schools
Bayview Avenue School of Arts & Sciences

325 W. Merrick Rd • Freeport, New York 11520
Phone 516-867-5255 • Fax 516-379-6906
Mary Garguilo, Principal – mgarguilo@freeportschools.org
Alma Rocha, Assistant Principal – arocha@freeportschools.org

"Where we are a family and learning is fun!"

Welcome to 2018/2019!

August 10, 2018

Dear Bayview Parents/Guardians:

It gives me great pleasure to welcome you to the Bayview Family and the **2018/2019** academic year! The faculty and staff join with me in eager anticipation of your child's arrival on **Tuesday, September 4, 2018 at 8:45 a.m.**

I trust that the following reminders will assist you as we approach the new school year:

- **Student Data Form** – Kindly complete the enclosed form **for each child** and return it to his/her teacher on **Tuesday, September 4, 2018.** Your cooperation in this matter will enable teachers to keep you informed about your child's academic progress and will also provide us with your contact information in the event of an emergency. **Please notify the main office regarding changes in your address as well as new home, work or mobile phone numbers.**
- **Join the PTA** – We also need your active support and involvement to guarantee the success of our PTA-sponsored special events. Your assistance will be valued and greatly appreciated.
- **Back-to-School Night** – Our faculty anticipates meeting with you to share academic expectations and classroom procedures on **Thursday, September 13, 2018 at 6:30 p.m.**
- **Bayview PTA Meeting** – **Monday, September 17, 2018 at 6:30 p.m.**
- **Bayview PTA Fall Pictures** – Individual and class pictures **Tuesday, September 25, 2018**
- **Bayview PTA PARP Kick-Off & Book Fair** – **Monday, September 24, 2018.** (Book fair through **09/27/18**)

We welcome your input and participation and will address your questions and concerns in a timely manner. Your active involvement has a direct impact on your child's success, so we encourage you to maintain open lines of communication with your child's teacher throughout the school year.

Thank you in advance for your support and cooperation. We look forward to building a productive home–school partnership to ensure your child's success. Should you have any questions or concerns, feel free to call us at 516-867-5255. We are here to serve you.

In partnership,

Mary Garguilo

Mary Garguilo
Principal

Escuelas Públicas de Freeport
Escuela Bayview Avenue de Artes & Ciencias
325 W. Merrick Rd • Freeport, New York 11520
Teléfono 516-867-5255 • Fax 516-379-6906
Mary Garguilo, Directora – mgarguilo@freeportschools.org
Alma Rocha, Asistente de la Directora – arocha@freeportschools.org

"¡Donde somos una familia y aprender es divertido!"

¡Bienvenidos a 2018/2019!

10 agosto del 2018

Estimados padres/representantes:

Me da un gran placer darles la bienvenida a la familia de Bayview y al nuevo Año Académico **2018/2019**. La facultad y todo el personal están preparándose ansiosamente para recibir a sus hijos el día **martes 4 de septiembre de 2018 a las 8:45 a.m.**

Confío en que los siguientes recordatorios le ayudarán a empezar el nuevo año escolar:

- **Formulario de Datos del Estudiante** – Se le ruega llenar el formulario de cada niño(a) y regresarlo a su maestra(o) el **4 de septiembre, 2018**. Su cooperación en este asunto ayudará a los maestros a mantenerle informado acerca del progreso académico de su hijo(a) y también nos proveerá con información importante en caso de emergencia. **Por favor notifique a la oficina de cualquier cambio de dirección, teléfono celular o del trabajo.**
- **Únase a PTA (Asociación de Padres y Maestros)** – Necesitamos su apoyo activo y su participación para garantizar el éxito de nuestra Asociación de Padres y Maestros y los eventos que ellos realizan. Su asistencia y colaboración serán apreciadas enormemente.
- **Noche de Regreso a la Escuela** – Nuestra facultad espera verlos para compartir sus expectativas y los procedimientos del aula de clases el **jueves 13 de septiembre de 2018 a las 6:30 p.m.**
- **Bayview PTA primer junta** – Lunes 17 de septiembre a las 6:30 p.m.
- **Bayview PTA Fotos de Otoño** – Individuales y de la clase **martes 25 de septiembre del 2018**
- **Bayview PTA Inicio de PARP y Feria de Libros** – Lunes 24 de septiembre del 2018 (Feria de libros hasta 27/09/17)

Como una escuela enfocada en la familia, valoramos su aportación y participación. Siempre trataremos de contestar sus preguntas e inquietudes lo más pronto posible. La participación de los padres impacta el éxito del estudiante, por lo tanto le rogamos que mantenga las líneas de comunicación abiertas con el maestro (a)de su hijo(a) todo el año.

Gracias de antemano, por su apoyo y cooperación. Esperamos poder construir una asociación de hogar-escuela que asegure el éxito de su hijo(a). Si tiene alguna pregunta o inquietud, por favor siéntase cómodo en llamarnos al 516-867-5255. Estamos aquí para servirle.

Como compañeros en la educación,

Mary Garguilo

Mary Garguilo
Directora

QUICK TIP 1: OPEN MULTIPLE CHANNELS OF COMMUNICATION!

Send home letters and write e-mails in multiple languages. If your district does robocalls, make sure they go out in multiple languages. Use interpreters, translators, and, with caution, translation software. Rather than simplify your message, amplify it and multiply it by using different modes and languages for communication.

How does your school make parents feel welcome from the day of registration? Whether a kindergartner's first day of school in September or a 6th grader's first day in mid-February, school routines and information about services should be available to parents, extended family members, or guardians. Some teachers like to have an informal survey available asking about parental preferences for contact (e-mail, text, phone, or postal mail) and others like to have goal-setting discussions, which are potential pathways for student learning. Some schools have parent advisory boards, which help inform the principal of successes and concerns, and other schools invite parents to volunteer in facilitated play (young children) or sports nights (older children).

Asking parents and active community members to volunteer is another key strategy to involve families in school-related activities, expand attendance at school events, find out about "best times" to schedule events, and recruit partners to support school programs through service and perhaps financially.

In other examples in which parental resources are highly valued—and parents and community members have strong ties to the school—we see parent–teacher-created Facebook pages and blogs as well as online newsletters, weekly school updates by e-mail, and invitations to be a mystery reader or career speaker. Another strong symbol of parent participation and cultural responsiveness in schools is having the cultural brokers establish Culture Corners. These corners (or parent centers) are set up in a prominent place in a school and offer cultural materials, information about local cultural events, and resources representative of students and their families. In other successful instances, schools offer parent centers run by bilingual parents. In a nutshell, the school becomes the community center of the neighborhood, where adults and children are welcome. Ross (2015) also suggests "adopting the community school model to provide critical wraparound services for students and families" (p. 3).

Another example of bidirectional family engagement (Delgado Gaitan, 2012) is when schools offer classes in English or job skills for parents on site. This creates concrete transactional support for improving the lives of families and, therefore, their children. Ross (2015) suggests that in order to support English learners, "a two-generation strategy" is essential to "close the language gap and expand opportunities" (p. 2). This means that families can provide academic support but must have the tools and strategies, which teachers can provide and model. Think about ways to prioritize family engagement at school and prioritize English learner training for teachers (Ross, 2015). Some of the recommendations that follow may be beyond the scope of any individual teacher's role and responsibility. Therefore, we recommend that you pull your resources and team up with your administrators and teacher leaders to campaign for collaborative practices in support of ELs:

➤ *Prioritize family engagement at school.* Develop a protocol for welcoming new families; set dates for checking in with families through home visits, phone calls, e-mails, or texts; design student-centered activities that invite parents to school; create a website with helpful school-related links; offer family nights where teachers model how to help your child with schoolwork; and host celebrations that highlight students' successes.

➤ *Prioritize English-learner training for teachers.* Offer (or, depending on your role, request and advocate for) ongoing professional development workshops on language acquisition; watch Teaching Channel videos on best practices for ELs; form a teachers' book club and read books from authors representing diverse cultural backgrounds; research successful language development programs; set yearly school-wide goals for supporting ELs; and participate visibly in community activities.

In your advocacy role as educator, be ready to speak to other teachers, families, and the larger community and answer questions as to why teamwork is needed to educate all students, particularly English learners. Share heart-warming and positive stories of successful collaborations. To build awareness and buy-in for collaboration, showcase projects or create minivideos of strategies parents can use at home, or deliverables developed from positive collaborations at school and community events. Create a parent center that becomes the welcoming hub for school and family programs and that responds to the needs of both students and the community. Alternatively, find out if there are parent organizations in community centers or local religious or cultural centers. Seek out opportunities to interact with parents and go where the conversations take place instead of waiting for the parents to come to school.

We often think of parents as having been to school, having school experiences, and knowing how to navigate school life. Invite the community to learn about how to use the latest version of Microsoft, Latin dancing, defensive driving to reduce your insurance cost, yoga, sports, and guitar lessons through continuing education. Current and relevant topics and skills are offered from district-sponsored workshops in the evening; encourage parents to take a break and try some. Would it surprise you to know that moms and dads account for 26 percent of the population of undergraduates trying to earn a college degree? This is an opportunity for teachers to see English learner parents as "parent learners" whether it be face to face, through online programs, or a combination of both. Parent learners may share feelings of invisibility and alienation (Horn, Salisbury, Ashburn, Schiener, & Pizer, 2018), and evening and weekend classes are a unique opportunity for schools to offer continuing education, classes in English, or college-level classes on site.

PARTNERSHIPS WITH COMMUNITY-BASED ORGANIZATIONS

Communities reflect the local families and the larger neighborhoods in which students live. Therefore, community partnerships may be new or already established relationships that support the community and have the capacity to help the schools. Community partnerships may be established with YMCAs, rotary clubs, faith-based associations, or the local neighborhood block association. Consider this: partnerships with community-based organizations will be unique to each community, and so will the joint activities designed in collaboration. After-school and summer programs are among the most popular ways that community-based organizations partner with schools and help extend learning opportunities through enrichment classes, courses, or summer camps. Sports, arts, music, and technology programs offered after school, during school breaks, and in the summer keep youngsters in the community while engaging them in meaningful language-building experiences. What organizations are open to partnering with your school? Which community-based organizations have a strong sense of actual connections to the community? You may have affiliations with police departments, fire stations, the chamber of commerce, or local area banks. Regardless of which institution participates, the partnerships should be student- and community-centered!

QUICK TIP 2: PLAN SHORT, HIGH-INTENSITY MEETINGS!

Try "sprints," defined as gatherings of people who work together for a short time to solve a problem. This approach steps away from the more traditional committee plan in which team members meet regularly. In a sprint, there are opportunities to work independently as well as with a group to solve a targeted problem. Ethan Bernstein, an associate professor from the Harvard Business School, suggests that "intermittently one might be better for complex problem solving" (HBS Communications, 2018, p. 1).

ENCOURAGING ADVOCACY AND PARENT LEADERSHIP

Parents know their children best! When we acknowledge that fact, we begin to build their leadership and advocacy skills. "By recasting parental involvement as civic engagement, inclusive educational leaders can join with parents to not only jettison the educational past but also to reimagine its present and future as affirming and transformational for all students and their families" (Horsford & Clark, 2015, p. 75). In your school community, look around and think about parents who are frequently at school, who have a voice (even in a whisper) in coordinating ideas and events, and ask them to springboard their work into a parent advisory board. This core group of parents can become proactive and help communicate the needs of English learners to other parents, the school, the larger district, and the community. Scanlan and Johnson (2015) remind us to take on the roles of "boundary spanners, border crossers, and advocates" (p. 165) on behalf of ELs. Let's unpack these ideas and recognize social boundaries that must be bridged to share power "with families and organizations beyond the schoolhouse doors, and to explore how [teachers'] educational goals for students intersect with the interests and goals of families and neighborhood residents" (p. 165). Advocacy begins with an interest in a common cause and a common voice to meet the needs of students.

Through the lens of civic engagement, many teachers will recall their own childhoods, where the school was the center of the community, the heart of the neighborhood. Having teachers and school personnel become active in local civic organizations helps to strengthen ties with the community. This is certainly not a new idea and has been championed by many educators (Fiore, 2016), but rather it is a reminder that grassroots efforts are often the most productive. Examples of active civic organizations that you can reach out to include the Girl Scouts, Boy Scouts, historical society, Chamber of Commerce, and the Salvation Army.

Additionally, organizations such as the PTA offer information on coalitions (a group of like-minded organizations). Often, coalitions can be established for a short-term reason (such as an election for a school board member) or long-term reasons (such as working to increase investments in education). Coalitions often have shared goals within their organizations and take an advocacy stance (such as calling for universal preK). In terms of English learners, advocacy may reflect a state's need and call for dual-language programs, a collective position on immigration or juvenile probation reform, or ensuring a piece of legislation is passed in a timely manner.

The work of Parent Teacher Student Associations (PTSAs) mirrors the work of PTAs but includes the students as having an important voice in representation. These are both formal organizations, and you likely have been a member as a student, as a parent, had your parents as a member, or are a member in your role as teacher. Parent leadership academies are an outgrowth of PTAs and help to build foundational leadership skills for parents.

Many of these programs are year-round and offer feedback to local school districts and offer educational workshops. Such workshops include relevant topics that are often requested by the parents themselves and have titles such as, "What Parents Need to Know" or "Everything You Always Wanted to Know About [_____]. For parents who are English learners, these educational opportunities may be how to access the library online, overcoming barriers to their child's education, or best strategies for reading at home with their youngster.

⏱ QUICK TIP 3: SEEK ADVICE!

Do you wonder how to best engage families when the adults do not communicate in English fluently? Establish an intercultural advisory board or family advisory committee that includes *brokering families*—those who speak both their native language and English—and intentionally create a bridge between more recently arrived families and the more established ones. In one school we supported, a bilingual teaching assistant assumed the most influential leadership role as the school community began to rely on her for her native language skills (of Tagalog) and her exceptional abilities to connect with families and community members, bring them to the school for events, and explain and clarify school-related matters that presented a special challenge to the growing Filipino community in the neighborhood.

MAKING SUCCESS WITH SCHOOL-PARENT-COMMUNITY PARTNERSHIPS VISIBLE

Success stories that are openly and frequently shared yield more success. How do you tell your story? The best stories we find are the ones in which parent activism and advocacy are highlighted. How are parents able to co-create solutions to improve the schools? In what ways are parents able to partner with teachers and seek authentic solutions to existing problems that relate to their own families?

In one suburban school with a large EL population, teachers created a full-service community school. The district had a "visionary commitment to educating the whole child and providing necessary services for its community" (Gomez, Ferrara, Santiago, Fanelli, & Taylor, 2012, p. 65). Of the many successful initiatives, The Second Cup of Coffee/La Segunda Taza de Café was developed specifically for parent education and capacity-building. The weekly forum was organized by the guidance center and offered parents workshops and discussion groups based on their preferences. The program strived to empower parents to become advocates for their children's education and increase participation and visibility for the parents of English learners.

In another "coffee" tale, teachers were concerned when parents were late dropping their children off to school. Many of the parents were new to the district and did not seem to understand the concept of "first period" or the importance of being on time, which is often culture-bound. In a co-created solution, the parents were offered a cup of hot coffee before the first bell as the students were brought to school. Attendance improved and the concept of early arrivals was met with smiles rather than yawns.

⏱ QUICK TIP 4: CREATE A COMMUNITY OF LEARNERS!

Form a learning community in which students, teachers, parents, and community members can belong. By creating a shared mission—with the purpose of connecting students', parents', teachers', and the communities' educational and cultural experiences—the center can be one of the "spokes of the wheel" in a neighborhood effort to value and honor local diversity. Give it an important title, perhaps with an informative acronym such as the COVE (Community Outreach to Value Education) Center. What a great way to advocate for inclusion of all neighborhood constituents and ensure they have a voice in the educational system!

 ## IN CONVERSATION WITH TEACHERS

We asked educators around the country the same question: How do you engage multilingual families in their children's education and schooling? As you read the responses, consider how they may be applicable to your own context.

Rob Greenhaw, instructional specialist with the Department of Migrant, English Learner, Immigrant, and Refugee Education, describes a family initiative he was leading when he worked at Confluence Academy South City, a public charter school in St. Louis, Missouri:

> *My ESOL team and I wanted a way to engage with our Spanish-speaking parents, make them feel welcome in our school, and show them we valued their language and culture. Leyendo con la Familia did just that. The program started in 2016 at Confluence Academy South City, a public charter school in St. Louis, Missouri, where 40 percent of the students are Hispanic. We invited parents to come to school during breakfast period and encouraged them to read with their kids in Spanish or English. District Title III funds covered the purchase of English-Spanish*

bilingual children's books, which fill bins set on library tables covered with colorful butcher paper. Parents enjoy coffee and donuts. At the end of each event, the kids receive a color copy of a Spanish-English bilingual book, which we print from a free website, to take home.

Leyendo con la Familia became popular. We held it in both the K–2nd and the 3rd–8th buildings on the first Tuesday and Thursday of each month. Soon we were averaging 25 families at each event. Our ESOL team began a bilingual book checkout program: each Wednesday, the K–2nd students selected books and swapped them for others the following week.

We're convinced Leyendo con la Familia has shown parents we want them as partners. It promotes literacy in the native language and helps them relate to our staff. Seeing parents and kids enjoy reading books in Spanish was one of the most rewarding aspects of my work at Confluence Academy South City. (To see a documentation of our work, go to https://www.youtube.com/watch?v=-2L1ORv_4Pg&t=108s.)

Elena Dokshansky, English-as-a-second-language (ESL) teacher in the Buffalo School District, New York, English language learner, and a mother of a multilingual child, shares her perspectives on building community relations across languages:

As an English language learner (ELL), ESL teacher, and a mother of a multilingual learner, I have always been a proponent of effective school–home collaboration! I was fortunate to begin my ESL teaching career in a school district with a majority of ELLs whose languages I spoke. It facilitated communication. Nevertheless, there were families missing school functions.

Having been an ELL, I was aware of numerous difficulties families experience adjusting to a new country and culture and not always having an opportunity to attend school events. Moreover, as a mother of a multilingual child, I knew about the value of constant communication with multilingual parents. In an effort to increase multilingual parent involvement, my school district was taking a number of collaborative steps that proved to bring positive change: (1) important communication was translated, (2) interpreters were used, (3) teachers had access to translated documents, and (4) parents were encouraged to communicate with the school in their native languages if they preferred to do so. The school district efforts were fruitful, and parental involvement increased! It was a collective effort of a school district and families!

Susan Blethen, Burlington High School teacher, shared the community partnership initiated by students in the International Club she moderated:

One of the best teaching experiences I have had in many years occurred when I worked with a community doctor and my students to create a safe space logo for our community. In 2017, a local doctor got in touch with the school to see if anyone would be interested in such a project. With the increase in anti-immigrant rhetoric, new Americans—refugees, immigrants, and asylum seekers—were distressed about their future in Burlington, Vermont, and the United States. What was going to happen to them? Would they be safe in America? Would they have to leave? Driven by the real fear she witnessed in her pediatric practice, Dr. Andrea Green reached out to

Burlington High School to see if she could support the students in feeling safe and welcome. The students of the International Club of Burlington High School were also worried and wanted to do something. The students met with Dr. Green in my classroom during their lunchtime to talk about these fears and ways to communicate that Vermont is a place where all are welcome.

During these meetings, an authentic design process began, and the students strengthened their voice and power to stand up against hurtful rhetoric. They Skyped with a local poet who had heard about the project and wanted to reach out to the students as well. They also worked with a local designer who volunteered his skills to polish the design the students created. Through this experience, the students were able to share how Burlington, Vermont, has been a welcoming community. It is a place without prejudice, where immigrants find peace, feel safe, and can live without fear—something they wanted to make visible to all. The final design the students created is an image of two hands supporting a dove (see Figure 5.3).

All Are Welcome Logo FIGURE 5.3

Although their focus was the immigrant community, the students chose #allarewelcome in English because they did not want anyone of any background, affiliation, or identity to feel excluded. Our small local project soon became a national one, as we were invited to share our story at the annual AMA (American Medical Association) convention for pediatricians and doctors from coast to coast who now wear the pins we made of the image. The image has been tweeted, Facebooked, and sent all over the nation. One of the highlights for the students came in April of 2017, when the club was invited by the Speaker of the House in Vermont to visit the senate and witness an immigrant protection bill. The students were greeted by lawmakers and press. They witnessed our govern-ment working to protect immigrant rights. Meaningful engagement with the community enhanced the learning and sense of belonging for this group of students. They became better speakers, and their self-esteem grew by leaps and bounds.

TECH TOOLBOX

It is important to consider the role of technology outside the classroom, especially from the point of view that our English learners are becoming global citizens and digital citizens. The question becomes, how do any of our emerging teams—student–student, teacher–student, or parent–student—develop techno-logical competencies that enhance language and education? "Dig-ital citizens should be able to distinguish between credible and untrustworthy news sources and sites; corroborate information across websites or accounts; contextualize stories; and under-stand the perspectives, methods, and evidence that authors use in multimodal texts" (Krutka & Carpenter, 2017, p. 53). English learners need to be able to understand social media as they learn to navigate the social and political hierarchies that they meet in school and in the larger community. Three tools that help students better understand social media content are Twitter, Shutterfly Share sites, and student-authored blogs.

TWITTER

Creating a Twitter handle for the local community to follow, for your intercultural advisory board, or for your school's learning community helps to share the message of intercultural respect and support. Within Twitter, you can share a quote, idea, or picture and retweet those to your Twitter followers. You can also tag others in your group or tweet links with clickable images that help spread the message of the community's events. A fun Twitter feature is "Moments," which allows you to combine images and tweets from multiple people into one story. This feature enables users to post brief celebrations, pictures of school-related successes, and videos. Social media is continually upgrading and changing and, at the same time, so strongly integrated in the social experience that it is a medium of importance that can benefit our English learners.

SHUTTERFLY SHARE SITES

Shutterfly Share sites are designed to exchange photos from your class, team, grade, advisory group, or community group and are excellent ways to communicate with parents who may not typically be home after school or in the early evening. There are both apps and websites that can be synced with others while you take, share, and view pictures. Let's say there is a fundraiser at a local bowling alley or a Saturday morning nature hike with a naturalist. Shutterfly Share sites allows you to post directions, make last minute updates in case of inclement weather, or use a discussion board within the community.

STUDENT-AUTHORED BLOGS

These have been around for about as long as the Internet. The concept of student-authored blogs has caught on, and students are writing in journal- or diary-style to share ideas or information. Blogger is one of the most popular blogging websites, but again this can change at any time, as social media is a quickly evolving, never-static set of forums. The reason to use student-authored blogs as part of the campaign to connect schools and communities is that bloggers tend to build relationships with their readers and many blogs allow for reader comments.

CONCLUSION

The essential building blocks for successful family–school–community partnerships are sustained collaboration, continuous learning for all, and coordinated support for students, teachers, and families. An important consideration for teachers is how to help parents become active participants while recognizing that families and communities have changed and continue to change. Collaborative efforts in bidirectional activities are integral in creating such partnerships. We encourage you to fire up and celebrate your successes and consider ways to optimize and prioritize family and community engagement at school. Your students will benefit!

Taking It Further: Reflection Questions

1. How do you make parents and community members feel comfortable when entering your school or district office?
2. How do you communicate about school events or ask for participation so that all parents and community members feel included?

3. How does the school or school district deal with controversial issues that may impact English learners and their families?

4. How do you fire up the community so that they become team members in the education of the community's children?

Additional Resources

Does your school have an active PTA, PTO (Parent Teacher Organization), or PTSA? There are so many acronyms and similar ideas, all derived from the guidelines offered by the National Parent Teacher Association. Visit www.pta.org for comprehensive information about partnerships and, while there, don't forget to check out the new resources on family engagement—https://www.pta.org/center-for-family-engagement.

Do you need a readily available resource for families to navigate the U.S. educational system? The National Clearinghouse for English Language Acquisition offers a multilingual resource for families to understand their child's educational choices. Visit https://ncela.ed.gov/family-toolkit.

Do you wonder where to find information about designing and implementing quality after-school programs? The After-school Alliance offers a comprehensive website for resources, research, advocacy, and technical assistance to after-school programs nationwide. Visit http://www.afterschoolalliance.org.

Are you interested in research and policy related to parent and community partnerships? The National Network of Partnership Schools at Johns Hopkins University, under the leadership of Dr. Joyce L. Epstein, offers current research and program models to develop parental engagement and community connections at the school, district, and state levels. Visit http://nnps.jhucsos.com.

CONCLUSION

So, why team up? What is so compelling about building collaborative partnerships? Gestalt psychologist Kurt Koffka stated, "The whole is other than the sum of the parts." If we use this phrase to frame our understanding of modern-day synergy, we can wholly buy into the idea that teams working together can achieve outcomes that could not be accomplished independently. This buy-in, in turn, creates a context for valuing each member of our classrooms, schools, and larger communities.

We strongly believe the pathway to success for English learners should be part of a caring, passionate, and proactive community that embraces diversity, risk taking, and advocacy. One of our personal and professional mottos is, "Use your power to empower others." Our hope is that this book provides the road map for empowering you to establish and maintain a thriving and collaborative approach to positive educational growth in your school community.

X marks the spot. You are here! Now put the book down, roll up your sleeves, and get to work! The signposts are clear; teamwork must take place in every classroom, in every school, and in every community:

When your students work in small and large groups and teams in the classroom, they create a vibrant community of learners.

 When successful partnerships emerge between students and teachers, trust, respect, and joint effort permeate the teaching-learning process.

 When teacher collaboration is the norm, a cohesive, coordinated, and cooperative (that's a lot of Cs) approach to serving English learners is achieved.

When your teams include members inside and outside of the school community, everyone benefits from the school-based and community-based assets.

Our ultimate goal? Empowered learners, teachers, parents, leaders, and communities! Demographic trends point to our ever-changing school populations as they continue to be more diverse and include more students of color as well as English learners. The future of ELs depends on our collective advocacy and team building that ensures the development of sustainable practices so that ELs and their families are well supported, feel valued, and thrive.

BIBLIOGRAPHY

Allensworth, E. M., Farrington, C. A., Gordon, M. F., Johnson, D. W., Klein, K., McDaniel, B., & Nagaoka, J. (2018). *Supporting social, emotional, and academic development: Research implications for educators*. Chicago, IL: University of Chicago Consortium on School Research.

Ashbrook, P. (2019). Discovering their sense of the world. *Science and Children, 56*(5), 18–19.

Banchi, H., & Bell, R. (2008). The many levels of inquiry. *Science and Children, 46*(2), 26–29.

Bonebright, D. A. (2010). 40 years of storming: A historical review of Tuckman's model of small group development. *Human Resource Development International, 13*, 111–120. doi:10.1080/13678861003589099

Boss, S. (2015). *Implementing project-based learning*. Bloomington, IN: Solution Tree.

Brown, S. (2010). Being an expert: Building social, cultural, and academic capital with an English learner. In A. Honigsfeld & A. Cohan (Eds.), *Breaking the mold of school instruction and organization: Innovative and successful practices for the twenty-first century*. Lanham, MD: Rowman & Littlefield.

Buckner, J. C. (2009). *Thinking maps: Path to proficiency for English language learners*. Cary, NC: Thinking Maps.

Burkins, J., & Yaris, K. (2013). Top ten themes of IRA Convention 2013. Retrieved from www.burkinsandyaris.com/top-ten-themes-of-ira-convention-2013/

Burns, D., & Darling-Hammond, L. (2014). *Teaching around the world: What can TALIS tell us*. Retrieved from https://edpolicy.stanford.edu/sites/default/files/publications/teaching-around-world-what-can-talis-tell-us_3.pdf

Cooper, A. (2012). 10 tips for teaching English-language learners. Retrieved from https://www.edutopia.org/blog/teaching-english-language-learners-ayanna-cooper

Cox-Petersen, A. (2011). *Educational partnerships: Connecting schools, families, and the community*. Thousand Oaks, CA: Sage.

Crawford, J. (2008). *Advocating for English learners: Selected essays.* Clevedon, UK: Multilingual Matters.

Cummins, J., & Early, M. (2015). *Big ideas for expanding minds: Teaching English language learners across the curriculum.* Toronto, Canada: Pearson.

Delgado Gaitan, C. (2012). Culture, literacy, and power in family–community–school–relationships. *Theory into Practice, 51,* 305–311.

DeLuca, C., Bolden, B., & Chan, J. (2017). Systemic professional learning through collaborative inquiry: Examining teachers' perspectives. *Teaching and Teacher Education, 67,* 67–78.

Dewey, J. (1938). *Experience and education.* New York: Collier.

Dodge, J., & Honigsfeld, A. (2014). *Core instructional routines: Go-to structures for effective literacy teaching, K–5.* Portsmouth, NH: Heinemann.

Dove, M. G., & Honigsfeld, A. (2018). *Co-teaching for English learners: A guide to collaborative planning, instruction, assessment, and reflection.* Thousand Oaks, CA: Corwin.

Dove, M. G., Honigsfeld, A., & Cohan, A. (2014). *Beyond core expectations: A schoolwide framework for serving the not-so-common learner.* Thousand Oaks, CA: Corwin.

DuFour, R. (2005). What is a professional learning community? In R. DuFour, R. Eaker, & R. DuFour (Eds.), *On common ground: The power of professional learning communities* (pp. 31–43). Bloomington, IN: Solution Tree.

DuFour, R., & DuFour, R. (2012*). The school leader's guide to professional learning communities at work.* Bloomington, IN: Solution Tree.

Dweck, C. S. (2007). *Mindset: The new psychology of success.* New York: Ballantine.

Eells, R. J. (2011). *Meta-analysis of the relationship between collective teacher efficacy and student achievement.* (Doctoral dissertation). Retrieved from http://ecommons.luc.edu/cgi/viewcontent.cgi?article=1132&context=luc_diss

Epstein, J. L., & Associates. (2019). *School, family, and community partnerships: Your handbook for action* (4th ed.). Thousand Oaks, CA: Corwin.

Facione, P., & Gittens, C. A. (2016). *Think critically* (3rd ed.). Boston: Pearson.

Ferlazzo, L. (2011). Involvement or engagement? *Educational Leadership, 68* (8), 10–14.

Fernandez Anderson, A. (2015). Engaging and effective strategies for English language learners. In D. Sisk (Ed.), *Accelerating and extending literacy for diverse students* (pp. 66–83). Lanham, MD: Rowman & Littlefield.

Fiore, D. J. (2016). *School-community relations.* New York: Routledge.

Frey, N., & Fisher, D. (2006). *Language arts workshop: Purposeful reading and writing instruction.* Upper Saddle River, NJ: Merrill Education.

Frey, N., & Fisher, D. (2013). *Rigorous reading: Five access points for comprehending complex texts.* Thousand Oaks, CA: Corwin.

Garcia, O., Ibarra Johnson, S., & Seltzer, K. (2017). *The translanguaging classroom: Leveraging student bilingualism for learning.* Philadelphia: Caslon.

Gibbons, P. (2015). *Scaffolding language scaffolding learning: Teaching English language learners in the mainstream classroom.* Portsmouth, NH: Heinemann.

Goldenberg, C. N., & Coleman, R. (2010). *Promoting academic achievement among English learners: A guide to the research*. Thousand Oaks, CA: Corwin.

Gomez, D. W., Ferrara, J., Santiago, E., Fanelli, F., & Taylor, R. (2012). Full-service community schools: A district's commitment to educating the whole child. In A. Honigsfeld & A. Cohan (Eds.), *Breaking the mold of education for culturally and linguistically diverse students: Innovative and successful practices for the 21st century* (pp. 65–73). Lanham, MD: Rowman & Littlefield.

Goodlad, J. L. (2004). *A place called school: Prospects for the future.* New York: McGraw-Hill.

Gottlieb, M., & Ernst-Slavit, G. (2014). *Academic language in diverse classrooms: Definitions and contexts.* Thousand Oaks, CA: Corwin.

Gottlieb, M., & Honigsfeld, A. (2019). From assessment of learning to assessment for and as learning. In Calderon, M. E., Dove, M. G., Staehr Fenner, D., Gottlieb, M., Honigsfeld, A., Ward Singer, T., & Zacarian, D. *Breaking down the wall: Essential shifts for English learners' success* (pp. 135–160). Thousand Oaks, CA: Corwin.

Gutiérrez, K., & Orellana, M. F. (2006). The "problem" of English learners: Constructing genres of difference. *Research in the Teaching of English, 40,* 502–507.

Hattie, J. (2009). *Visible learning: A synthesis of over 800 meta-analyses relating to achievement.* New York: Routledge.

Hattie, J. (2012). *Visible learning for teachers: Maximizing impact on learning.* New York: Routledge.

Hattie, J. (2015). *What works best in education: The politics of collaborative expertise.* Retrieved from https://www.pearson.com/content/dam/corporate /global/pearson-dot-com/files/hattie/150526_ExpertiseWEB_V1.pdf

Hattie, J. (2018). Collective Teacher Efficacy (CTE). Retrieved from https:// visible-learning.org/2018/03/collective-teacher-efficacy-hattie/

HBS Communications (2018, August 15). Problem-solving techniques take on new twist. *The Harvard Gazette.* Retrieved from https://news.harvard. edu/gazette/story/2018/08/collaborate-on-complex-problems-but-only-intermittently/

Helman, L., Rogers, C., Frederick, A., & Struck, M. (2016). *Inclusive literacy in teaching: Differential approaches in multilingual elementary classrooms.* New York: Teachers College Press.

Honigsfeld, A., & Cohan, A. (2015). *Serving English language learners.* San Diego, CA: Bridgepoint.

Honigsfeld, A., & Dove, M. G. (2019). *Collaborating for English learners: A foundational guide to integrated practices* (2nd ed.). Thousand Oaks, CA: Corwin.

Horn, M. B., Salisbury, A. D., Ashburn, E., Schiener, J., & Pizer, L. (2018). *Parent learners: Insights for innovation.* Retrieved from https://tinyurl. com/y9rk66o5

Horsford, S. D., & Clark, C. (2015). Inclusive leadership and race. In G. Theoharis & M. Scanlan (Eds.), *Leadership for increasingly diverse schools* (pp. 58–81). New York: Routledge.

Ishimaru, A. M., Torres, E. K., Salvador, J. E., Lott, J., Cameron Williams, D. M., & Tran, C. (2016). Reinforcing deficit, journeying toward equity: Cultural brokering in family engagement initiatives. *American Educational Research Journal, 53*, 850–882.

Jensen, E. (2013). *Engaging students with poverty in mind: Practical strategies for raising achievement.* Alexandria, VA: ASCD.

Kagan, S., & Kagan, M. (2009). *Kagan cooperative learning.* San Clemente, CA: Kagan Publishing.

Kagan, S., & Kagan, M. (2015). *Kagan cooperative learning.* San Clemente, CA: Kagan Publishing.

Kagan, S., Kagan, M., & Kagan, L. (2016). *59 Kagan structures: Proven engagement strategies.* San Clemente, CA: Kagan Publishing.

Kendall, J. (2006). Small group instruction for English language learners: It makes sense. *Principal Leadership, 6*(6), 28–31.

Kieffer, M., Lesaux, N., Rivera, M., & Francis, D. (2009). Accommodations for English language learners taking large-scale assessments: A meta-analysis on effectiveness and validity. *Review of Educational Research, 79,* 1168–1201.

Krutka, D. G., & Carpenter, J. P. (2017). Digital citizenship in the curriculum. *Educational Leadership, 75*(3), 50–55.

Ladson-Billings, G. (1995). Toward a theory of culturally relevant pedagogy. *American Educational Research Journal, 32,* 465–491.

Ladson-Billings, G. (2014). Culturally relevant pedagogy 2.0: a.k.a. the remix. *Harvard Educational Review, 84*(1), 74–84.

Larmer, J. (2015). Gold standard PBL: Essential project design elements [blog post]. Retrieved from http://www.bie.org/blog/gold_standard_pbl_essential_project_design_elements

Larmer, J. (2016). It's a project-based world. *Educational Leadership, 73*(6), 66–70.

Larmer, J., Mergendoller, J., & Boss, S. (2015). *Setting the standard for project-based learning: A proven approach to rigorous classroom instruction.* Alexandria, VA: ASCD.

Lent, R. C. (2016). *This is disciplinary literacy: Reading, writing, thinking, and doing … content area by content area.* Thousand Oaks, CA: Corwin.

Levine, P. (2016). The question each citizen must ask. *Educational Leadership, 73*(6), 30–34.

Lewis, C., & Hurd, J. (2011). *Lesson study step by step: How teacher learning communities improve instruction.* Portsmouth, NH: Heinemann.

Mapp, K. L. (2003). Having their say: Parents describe why and how they are engaged in children's learning. *School Community Journal, 13*(1), 35–64.

Marzano, R. J., Warrick, P. B., Rains, C. L., & DuFour, R. (2018). *Leading a high-reliability school.* Bloomington, IN: Solution Tree.

Maslow, A. H. (1999). *Toward a psychology of being* (3rd ed.). New York: Wiley & Sons.

McDermott, C. L., & Honigsfeld, A. (2017). Preparing science teachers for project-based, integrated, collaborative instruction. In L. C. de Oliveira &

K. Campbell Wilcox (Eds.), *Teaching science to English language learners* (pp. 59–81). Cham, Switzerland: Palgrave Macmillan.

Moll, L., Amanti, C., Neff, D., & Gonzalez, N. (1992). Funds of knowledge for teaching: Using a qualitative approach to connect homes and classrooms. *Theory into Practice, 31,* 132–141.

National Education Association (NEA). (2015). *How educators can advocate for English language learners: All in!* Washington, DC: Author.

Ohta, A. (2001). *Second language acquisition processes in the classroom: Learning Japanese.* Mahwah, NJ: Lawrence Erlbaum Associates.

Paris, D. (2012). Culturally sustaining pedagogy: A needed change in stance, terminology, and practice. *Educational Researcher, 41*(3), 93–97.

Paris, D., & Alim, H. S. (2017). *Culturally sustaining pedagogies: Teaching and learning for justice in a changing world.* New York: Teachers College Press.

Pearson, P. D., & Gallagher, M. C. (1983). The instruction of reading comprehension. *Contemporary Educational Psychology, 8,* 317–344.

Perkins-Gough, D. (2015). Secrets of the teenage brain: A conversation with Frances E. Jensen, *Educational Leadership, 73,* 16–20.

Rechtachaffen, D. (2014). *The way of mindful education.* New York: Norton.

Ross, T. (2015). *The case for a two-generation approach for educating English language learners.* Washington, DC: Center for American Progress Retrieved from www.americanprogress.org

Rowan, J. (1998). Maslow amended. *The Journal of Humanistic Psychology, 38*(1), 81–92. doi:10.1177/00221678980381008

Ryan, C. (2013). *Language use in the United States: 2011.* Retrieved from https://www.census.gov/library/publications/2013/acs/acs-22.html

Scanlan, M., & Johnson, L. (2015). Inclusive leadership on the social frontiers: Family and community engagement. In M. Scanlan, & G. Theoharis (Eds.), *Leadership for increasingly diverse schools* (pp. 162–185). New York: Routledge.

Schmoker, M. (2009). What money can't buy: Powerful, overlooked opportunities for learning. *Kappan, 90,* 524–527.

Short, K. (2018). *More talking in class, please.* Retrieved from https://www.edutopia.org/article/more-talking-class-please

Soto, I. (2014). *Moving from spoken to written language with ELLs.* Thousand Oaks, CA: Corwin.

Sousa, D. (2016). *How the brain learns.* Thousand Oaks, CA: Corwin.

Staehr Fenner, D. (2013a). *Advocating for English learners: A guide for educators.* Thousand Oaks, CA: Corwin.

Staehr Fenner, D. (2013b). *Implementing the Common Core State Standards for English learners: The changing role of the ESL teacher.* Alexandria, VA: TESOL International Association. Retrieved from http://www.tesol.org/docs/default-source/advocacy/ccss_convening_final-8-15-13.pdf?sfvrsn=8

Suarez-Orozco, C., & Suarez-Orozco, M. M. (2001). *Children of immigration.* Cambridge, MA: Harvard University Press.

Takanishi, R., & Menestral, S. L. (Eds.). (2017). *Promoting the educational success of children and youth learning English: Promising futures.* Washington, DC: The National Academies Press. doi:10.17226/24677

Thousand, J. S., Villa, R. A., & Nevin, A. I. (2015). *Differentiating instruction: Planning for universal design and teaching for college and career readiness* (2nd ed.). Thousand Oaks, CA: Corwin.

Tomlinson, C. A. (2001). *How to differentiate instruction in mixed-ability classrooms* (2nd ed.). Alexandria, VA: ASCD.

Tomlinson, C. A. (2003). *Fulfilling the promise of the differentiated classroom: Strategies and tools for responsive teaching.* Alexandria, VA: ASCD.

Tough, P. (2012). *How children succeed: Grit, curiosity, and the hidden power of character.* New York: Houghton Mifflin Harcourt.

Tuckman, B. W. (1965). Developmental sequence in small groups. *Psychological Bulletin, 63*, 384–399.

Tung, R. (2013). Innovations in educational equity for English language learners. [Special Issue]. *Voices in Urban Education, 37.* Retrieved from http://vue.annenberginstitute.org/issues/37/innovations-educational-equity-english-language-learners

U.S. Department of Justice & U.S. Department of Education. (2015). Dear colleague letter. Retrieved from https://www2.ed.gov/about/offices/list/ocr/letters/colleague-el-201501.pdf

U.S. Department of Education, Office of English Language Acquisition (OELA). (2017). Fast Facts. Languages spoken by English learners (ELs). Retrieved from https://ncela.ed.gov/files/fast_facts/FastFactsAllLanguagesFebruary2017.pdf

Valdés, G. (2004). Between support and marginalization: The development of academic language in linguistic minority children. *Bilingual Education and Bilingualism, 7*(2&3), 102–132.

Vangrieken, K., Dochy, F., Raes, E., & Kyndt, E. (2015). Teacher collaboration: A systematic review. *Educational Research Review, 15*, 17–40.

Washington State Board of Education. (2018). 2018–23 SBE strategic plan. Retrieved from https://www.sbe.wa.gov/sites/default/files/public/documents/StratPlan/SBE%20Draft%20Strategic%20Plan%20Draft%2010.9.18.pdf

WIDA. (2014). *The WIDA standards framework and its theoretical foundations.* Retrieved from https://wida.wisc.edu/sites/default/files/resource/WIDA-Standards-Framework-and-its-Theoretical-Foundations.pdf

Zacarian, D. (2013). *Mastering academic language: A framework for supporting student achievement.* Thousand Oaks, CA: Corwin.

Zacarian, D., & Silverstone, M. (2015). *In it together: How students, family, and community partnerships advance engagement and achievement in diverse classrooms.* Thousand Oaks, CA: Corwin.

Zhang, J., Niu, C., Munawar, S., & Anderson, R. C. (2016). What makes a more proficient discussion group in English language learners' classrooms? Influence of teacher talk and student backgrounds. *Research in the Teaching of English, 51,* 183–208.

Zwiers, J. (2014). *Building academic language: Meeting Common Core Standards across disciplines, Grades 5–12* (2nd ed.). San Francisco: Jossey-Bass.

INDEX

Note: The letter *f* following a page number denotes a figure.

ABOUT THE AUTHORS

Audrey Cohan, EdD, is senior dean for research and scholarship at Molloy College, Rockville Centre, New York. During her 25-year tenure at Molloy College, she has served as professor, chair of the Education Department, and interim dean for the Division of Natural Sciences. Cohan has taught in the undergraduate and graduate programs and is currently teaching critical issues at the doctoral level for the EdD Program.

She began her career as a special education teacher in New York City, working with students with special needs in both self-contained and resource-room settings. Her first book—*Sexual Harassment and Sexual Abuse: A Handbook for Teachers and Administrators*—published in 1995, was an outgrowth of her dissertation work, which focused on child sexual abuse within schools. Along with Andrea Honigsfeld, Cohan co-edited a five-volume *Breaking the Mold* series about educational innovation. Additionally, as a New York State-certified special education and TESOL instructor, she has published numerous peer-reviewed articles about English language learners, including "Differentiating Between Learning Disabilities and Typical Second Language Acquisition: A Case Study" and "Piloting a Pre-referral Data Collection Tool: A Documentary Account." The textbook *Serving English Language Learners*, published in 2016, earned the Textbook & Academic Authors Association (TAA) Most Promising New Textbook Award. Her other book publications include *Beyond Core Expectations: A Schoolwide Framework for Serving the Not-So-Common Learner* (2014) and *John Dewey: America's Peace-Minded Educator* (2016). While at Molloy College, Cohan has received the Faculty Leadership Award, the Faculty Recognition Award, the Molloy College Research Award, and the Distinguished Service Award.

Andrea Honigsfeld, EdD, is associate dean and professor in the School of Education and Human Services at Molloy College, Rockville Centre, New York. She directs a doctoral program in Educational Leadership for Diverse Learning Communities. Before entering the field of teacher education, she was an English-as-a-foreign-language teacher in Hungary (grades 5–8 and adult) and an English-as-a-second-language teacher in New York City (grades K–3 and adult). She also taught Hungarian at New York University.

Honigsfeld received a doctoral fellowship at St. John's University, New York, where she conducted research on individualized instruction and learning styles. She has published extensively on working with English language learners and offering a collaborative approach to serving ELs. She received a Fulbright Award to lecture in Iceland in the fall of 2002. Since 2001, she has been presenting at conferences across the United States, Canada, Denmark, Great Britain, Sweden, the Philippines, Thailand, and the United Arab Emirates. She frequently offers staff development, primarily focusing on effective differentiated strategies and collaborative practices for English-as-a-second-language and general-education teachers. She coauthored *Differentiated Instruction for At-Risk Students* (2009) and co-edited the five-volume *Breaking the Mold of Education* series (2010–2013) with Audrey Cohan. She is also the coauthor of *Core Instructional Routines: Go-To Structures for Effective Literacy Teaching, K–5 and 6–12* (2014). Along with Maria G. Dove, she co-edited *Coteaching and Other Collaborative Practices in the EFL/ESL Classroom: Rationale, Research, Reflections, and Recommendations* (2012) and coauthored *Collaboration and Co-Teaching: Strategies for English Learners* (2010), *Common Core for the Not-So-Common Learner, Grades K–5: English Language Arts Strategies* (2013), *Common Core for the Not-So-Common Learner, Grades 6–12: English Language Arts Strategies* (2013), *Collaboration and Co-Teaching: A Leader's Guide* (2015), *Coteaching for English Learners: A Guide to Collaborative Planning, Instruction, Assessment, and Reflection* (2018), *Collaborating for English Learners: Foundational Guide to Integrated Practices* (2019)—five of which are best-sellers. With Audrey Cohan and Maria G. Dove, she coauthored *Beyond Core Expectations: A Schoolwide Framework for Serving the Not-So-Common Learner* (2014).

Maria G. Dove, EdD, is professor in the School of Education and Human Services at Molloy College, Rockville Centre, New York, where she teaches preservice and inservice teachers about the research and best practices for developing effective programs and school policies for English learners. Before entering the field of higher education, she worked for more than 30 years as an English-as-a-second-language teacher in public school settings (grades K–12) and in adult English language programs in Nassau County, New York.

In 2010, Dove received the Outstanding ESOL Educator Award from New York State Teachers of English to Speakers of Other Languages (NYS TESOL). She frequently provides professional development for educators throughout the United States on the teaching of diverse students. She also serves as a mentor for new ESOL teachers, as well as an instructional coach for general education teachers and literacy specialists. She has published articles and book chapters on collaborative teaching practices, instructional leadership, and collaborative coaching. With Andrea Honigsfeld, she coauthored six best-selling books— *Collaboration and Co-Teaching: Strategies for English Learners* (2010), *Common Core for the Not-So-Common Learner, Grades K–5: English Language Arts Strategies* (2013), and *Common Core for the Not-So-Common Learner, Grades 6–12: English Language Arts Strategies* (2013), *Collaboration and Co-Teaching: A Leader's Guide* (2015), *Co-Teaching for English Learners: A Guide to Collaborative Planning, Instruction, Assessment, and Reflection* (2018), and *Collaborating for English Learners: Foundational Guide to Integrated Practices* (2019)—and co-edited *Coteaching and Other Collaborative Practices in the EFL/ESL Classroom: Rationale, Research, Reflections, and Recommendations* (2012). With Andrea Honigsfeld and Audrey Cohan she coauthored *Beyond Core Expectations: A Schoolwide Framework for Serving the Not-So-Common Learner* (2014).

RELATED ASCD RESOURCES

At the time of publication, the following resources were available (ASCD stock numbers appear in parentheses):

Print Products

Success with Multicultural Newcomers & English Learners: Proven Practices for School Leadership Teams by Margarita Espino Calderón and Shawn Slakk (#117026)

Beyond Co-Teaching Basics: A Data-Driven, No-Fail Model for Continuous Improvement by Wendy W. Murawski and Wendy W. Lochner (#118007)

Classroom Instruction That Works with English Language Learners, 2nd Edition by Jane D. Hill and Kirsten B. Miller (#114004)

Classroom Instruction That Works with English Language Learners Facilitator's Guide by Jane D. Hill and Cynthia L. Björk (#108052)

Classroom Instruction That Works with English Language Learners Participant's Workbook by Jane D. Hill and Cynthia L. Björk (#108053)

Getting Started with English Language Leaners: How Educators Can Meet the Challenge by Judie Haynes (#106048)

The Language-Rich Classroom: A Research-Based Framework for Teaching English Language Learners by Persida Himmele and William Himmele (#108037)

Reaching Out to Latino Families of English Language Learners by David Campos, Rocio Delgago, and Mary Esther Soto Huerta (#110005)

Strategies for Success with English Language Learners: An ASCD Action Tool by Virginia Pauline Rohas (#111061)

Teaching in Tandem: Effective Co-Teaching in the Inclusive Classroom by Gloria Lodato Wilson and Joan Blednick (#110029)

Co-Planning for Co-Teaching: Time-Saving Routines That Work in Inclusive Classrooms (ASCD Arias) by Gloria Lodato Wilson (#SF117018)

Teacher Teamwork: How do we make it work? (ASCD Arias) by Margaret Searle and Marilyn Swartz (#SF115045)

Productive Group Work: How to Engage Students, Build Teamwork, and Promote Understanding by Nancy Frey, Douglas Fisher, and Sandi Everlove (#109018)

Teaching English Language Learners Across the Content Areas by Judie Haynes and Debbie Zacarian (#109032)

For up-to-date information about ASCD resources, go to www.ascd.org. You can search the complete archives of *Educational Leadership* at www.ascd.org/el.

ASCD myTeachSource®

Download resources from a professional learning platform with hundreds of research-based best practices and tools for your classroom at http://myteachsource.ascd.org/.

For more information, send an e-mail to member@ascd.org; call 1-800-933-2723 or 703-578-9600; send a fax to 703-575-5400; or write to Information Services, ASCD, 1703 N. Beauregard St., Alexandria, VA 22311-1714 USA.

WHOLE CHILD
TENETS

The ASCD Whole Child approach is an effort to transition from a focus on narrowly defined academic achievement to one that promotes the long-term development and success of all children. Through this approach, ASCD supports educators, families, community members, and policymakers as they move from a vision about educating the whole child to sustainable, collaborative actions.

Team Up, Speak Up, Fire Up! relates to the **safe, engaged, supported,** and **challenged** tenets.
For more about the ASCD Whole Child approach, visit www.ascd.org/wholechild.

1 HEALTHY
Each student enters school healthy and learns about and practices a healthy lifestyle.

2 SAFE
Each student learns in an environment that is physically and emotionally safe for students and adults.

3 ENGAGED
Each student is actively engaged in learning and is connected to the school and broader community.

4 SUPPORTED
Each student has access to personalized learning and is supported by qualified, caring adults.

5 CHALLENGED
Each student is challenged academically and prepared for success in college or further study and for employment and participation in a global environment.